MINDSET TRAINING
CONQUER YOUR MIND AND THE REST WILL FOLLOW

DR. NEKESHIA HAMMOND

Copyright © 2024 by Dr. Nekeshia Hammond

All rights reserved.

No part of this book may be reproduced in any form or by any electronic or mechanical means, including information storage and retrieval systems, without written permission from the author, except for the use of brief quotations in a book review.

ISBN: 979-8-9877574-9-9

CONTENTS

Foreword	vii

PART ONE
AN UNDERSTANDING

1. Abundance Vs. Scarcity	3
2. Self-Care	7
3. Self-Care Is Not Selfish	13

PART TWO
MENTAL SELF-CARE

4. Positive Self-Talk	21
5. Clearing Your Mental Clutter	25
6. Mindset Training	29
7. Inner Peace	35
8. Permission to Heal	41

PART THREE
PHYSICAL SELF-CARE

9. Nutrition, Movement, and Sleep	49

PART FOUR
EMOTIONAL SELF-CARE

10. Mindfulness Practices	59
11. The Value of Relationships	65
12. Prevention vs. Intervention	69
13. Self-Love	77
14. Mental Health Detox	81

PART FIVE
SPIRITUAL SELF-CARE

15. Spiritual Growth	89
16. Giving Back is Good for Your Mental Health	93
17. Gratitude	101
18. Helping Others	107

PART SIX
CONCLUSION

19. Lifetime Commitment	119
20. Therapy Options	125
21. The Seed	131
About the Author	135
Acknowledgments	137
Resources	139
Support groups	143

To my late mentor who believed in me so much,
Yusuf Salaam.
I miss you every day.
Thank you for everything you taught me.

It brings me great delight to be tasked with writing the foreword for someone I have so much respect for. I've known Dr. Nekeshia Hammond for several years now. When I first met her years ago, I knew that she was different. Have you ever met someone and from the first encounter you can feel the magnitude of their presence, and sense their genuine heart and spirit? That was my experience with Nekeshia several years ago.

In the world we live in today there are so many self-proclaimed gurus giving advice and writing books, and you often wonder, are they credible? Do they really care, and do they really know what they're talking about? Well I can tell you, Dr. Hammond, she is what I'd call "The Real Deal." She's been speaking for over a decade on the topic of mental health, self-care and wellness. She's been a constant advocate for youth and adults in the mental health space. In addition to that she has owned her successful practice for over 15 years! She's been doing what I call, life changing and life giving work for a very long time. Not only that, but she's been doing it at the highest level.

Being her speaking coach, and business mentor, I've had the privilege of sharing the stage with her several times. Every time she speaks her message is in alignment with her calling and purpose which is to shine a light and educate those listening on the importance of mental wellness. I recall in April of 2022, I flew to Miami and witnessed her give a powerful TEDx speech on the importance of mental wellness. Out of all the speakers that presented on the TEDx stage, hers was the most captivating presentation. I watched closely how she navigated the stage with confidence and grace as the audience held on to her every word. It was quite the experience!

Dr. Hammond's greatness has excelled past her vast and successful career of speaking and mental health treatment. I've witnessed her receive multiple awards on stage at events for her speaking, leadership, and Spirit of Excellence. In addition to this, she's one of the most generous people I know. I've spoken to several people over the years who have told me that Dr. Hammond secretly paid for their flights and hotel rooms so that they're able to attend various conferences and events. What's most impressive is that she did so without anyone knowing. To those of us who know her, this doesn't surprise us at all. What rivals her brilliant mind is her compassionate heart and genuine care for others.

Taking into full consideration who Dr. Nekeshia Hammond really is, I can't express enough how excited I am that you picked up this book!! Within the pages of this book you're going to learn all about the growth mindset, self care, and how you can grow physically, mentally, emotionally, and spiritually.

Some of you may be thinking *"eh...my life isn't that bad."* And you're right. Maybe it's just ok. Or maybe for you life's been good, but you aspire for it to be better? We all know by now that life isn't about what happens to us, but more so how we respond and react to it. Nowadays the term "self care" or "mental health" seems to be these popular buzz words, but in reality what we're talking about is quality of life.

A life well lived, is a life filled with purpose, and peace. This is what you deserve! You deserve to be happy. You deserve to have joy and peace. You deserve to live a fulfilled and prosperous life, and if you apply the teachings that she provides in this book, you can expect to live the life that you deserve!

If you're looking to take your life to new heights it's imperative that you read this book, and implement the principles provided. Think about it this way, not only will this book enhance your life, but those directly connected to you as well. Ask yourself....who will benefit from you being the best version of yourself? I believe the next level of your life lies within the pages of this book. Enjoy the book, and enjoy the enhanced life that will evolve from it.

- Jeremy Anderson

PART ONE
AN UNDERSTANDING

"Your well-being fuels your success. Find harmony in the chaos, and thrive!"

— DR. NEKESHIA HAMMOND

CHAPTER ONE
ABUNDANCE VS. SCARCITY

"Self-care is how you take your power back."

— LALAH DELIA

IF YOU TAKE CARE OF SOMETHING, ANYTHING — BETTER, IT WILL BE BETTER, perform better, taste better, run smoother and faster, fly higher, grow stronger, dive deeper, etc. Caring for something is the best way to get the best out of it. Athletes take care of their bodies to get maximum results in their field of play, singers take care of their throats and voices for optimal sounds, professional mechanics take care of their sports cars so they go as fast as possible, and gardeners care for their vegetables for maximum ripeness and flavor.

The proper care for something is critical. If the bees don't care for sunflowers and bring pollen from one to the other, they cannot form seeds and reproduce. Conversely, poor or little care of something can stifle its growth, kill its potential, and rob the world of the benefits it can provide.

Essentially, whatever you take better care of is just... better!

I wrote this book so that you can take better care of... you!

One of the problems plaguing humanity is that people don't know how or don't know that they need to care for themselves. There are far too many people who think poorly of themselves. Maybe, as children, they were born into poverty, grew up in an abusive environment, lived lavishly with excessive wealth but felt that their parents didn't have time for them, were indoctrinated into an oppressive religion, lost their parents or a parent, or were bullied. Whatever the reason, and they vary from individual to individual, negative self-thinking is destroying the quality of life they have the potential to live.

Anxiety is at an all-time high. There's even a medical term for it – generalized anxiety disorder (GAD). Anxiety comes in many forms, whether it's social anxiety, which affects people more specifically in social situations, or their very self-conscious, perhaps not wanting to eat in front of others, or they fear people are talking about them, worry they get lost in a crowd, don't feel equipped to handle the rigors of the day, etc.

Too many people are living lackluster lives because they feel overwhelmed. You may have no idea that someone you know struggles mentally every day to get out of bed. They lie awake, trying to go back to sleep, silence their phones, dreading having to leave their room and face another day.

Then there are those who lack clarity. They have a zest for life, a feeling that they were meant for more, but they don't know what it is. They constantly look for places to put their energies but whatever they do doesn't give them the fulfillment they yearn for. It's like they live their lives with their gas tank always at a quarter tank.

The battle between living a life you're proud of or one you loathe, dear reader, is between your ears. Mindset can be categorized in two ways: Abundance and Scarcity. An abundance mindset – an innate feeling that no matter what, everything will work out for your good. People with an abundance mindset favor personal and spiritual growth. Self-help guru Tony Robbins says an abundance mindset is the belief that there are enough resources in the world for everyone – and of being grateful for whatever God or the universe provides. They don't have time to be jealous of another person's success; they're too busy working on reaching their goals. They are fun to be around because they believe life happens for them, not against them.

Then there's the scarcity mindset. People suffering from this mindset are rarely happy for long periods of time. They're constantly expecting bad, undesirable, or damaging things to happen to them. Unknowingly, they negatively impact the people closest to them, whether it's their spouse, children, family members, or close friends. They don't like their job or career. They get angry quickly; when grief strikes, it takes a long time for it to leave, and they have work-life-balance issues. They lack self-confidence and shy away from trying new things, limiting the many beautiful experiences life provides.

I've had the honor of traveling throughout the United States and many countries. I've been privileged to speak to groups of thousands, hundreds, and many people one-on-one. I've spoken to people of all walks of life, religions, ethnicities, and social status. While people's religious beliefs, political beliefs, food choices, and entertainment choices differ – the same mental battle goes on in every individual. I've seen many people change their mindsets, which changed their lives. I've cried happy tears with someone who told me they never thought they could be so fulfilled.

Contained in this book are answers you've been searching for, including the ones to questions you didn't know to ask. I have taken my 15 years as a psychologist and my experiences of working with more people than I can count and put them into practical, real-world tips and advice you can implement immediately to start to live a better life. Whether you're ready to take a giant leap and radically change your life, or you're willing to take baby steps to improve your quality of life, I have packed plenty of inspiration, motivation, and the mindset tools necessary to live the life you've always wanted.

I recommend you grab a Sharpie or a pen. There will be plenty of content that will speak to you, speak to your situation, speak to your mind and soul – and you'll want to highlight them to ensure you don't just get motivated or enlightened but that you grasp the teachings and they become part of the fabric that makes you the amazing human being you were put on this earth to become.

You do know you are amazing, right?

You do know that you are meant to do more than you're doing now, right?

You do know that you have it in you to live the life of your dreams, right?

If you allow me to guide you with this book through the murky waters of a healthy mindset, I promise you that your life will change for the better. That, my friend, is a journey worth taking.

Do you have your Sharpie? Are you ready to take notes?

Awesomeness.

Let us begin...

CHAPTER TWO
SELF-CARE

"In dealing with those who are undergoing great suffering, if you feel 'burnout' setting in, if you feel demoralized and exhausted, it is best, for the sake of everyone, to withdraw and restore yourself. The point is to have a long-term perspective."

— THE DALAI LAMA

A LOT OF TIMES WHEN PEOPLE THINK OF SELF-CARE, THEY THINK THEY NEED A lot of money or a lot of time, or need to make a huge commitment and drastically change their lives. Well, here's the reality: There's a lot of self-care that you can do that's free. There's a lot of self-care that you can do that's fun. There's self-care that you can do by yourself or with your family and your friends. In this chapter I'm going to discuss different ways that you can incorporate self-care into your life. I am not ashamed to say I used to SUCK at self-care with a capital "S."

I used to not focus on myself and just run myself RAGGED. I had all these responsibilities, all these involvements and so many different things "to do" it seemed. I was playing so many different roles, and wasn't paying attention to my mental health or my physical health. The problem is, it's not sustainable to not take care of yourself for long periods of time. It absolutely is not. Burnout is a real thing, but what happened to me over time was after I hit burnout. I saw how critically important it was to make a commitment to self-care. If I wanted to change who I was, and if I wanted to show up as the best version of who I could be for myself and also for those around me, I needed to change.

I would tell myself that if I want to show up as the best version of myself, I had to make sure that I took care of me and that meant more than getting a mani/pedi once in a while. I had to make sure that I was doing what I needed to do to commit and put myself first for my own mental health.

Make a commitment to self-care.

I know that it may sound scary, but you have to make the commitment to self-care, meaning taking care of you and putting yourself first. I've talked extensively about self-care on my *Mental Health Moment with Dr. Hammond* live streams (you can find replays on Dr. Nekeshia Hammond YouTube page). I remember during one of my *Mental Health Moments* when someone asked on the live show: "How can you focus on only yourself? What about selflessness?" Well, here's the thing to remember: Self-care is NOT selfish. Instead, what it means when you put yourself first is you're actually putting yourself first to become the best version of who you are, so you can show up to be the best version of who you are in any role that you're playing in life.

Make this commitment now. It takes baby steps sometimes. Maybe you're the type of person that wants to take leaps all the time. However, it can be rather exhausting to constantly be thinking about how you make leaps into doing things. Leaps are important, yes, but you also want to think about how you can take these baby steps for self-care.

Maybe it's overwhelming for you to think about, right? Let me put self-care on a higher priority. Let me do daily self-care. Now, daily self-care might sound overwhelming to you. However, if you think about it, what can you commit to do right now? Once a week? What can you commit to do once a week? What can you commit to do once a month? What is realistic for you? The reality is every single one of us has time to dedicate to self-care. Every single one of us.

I can honestly say to you, as I write this book, that I am exercising more than I ever have in my life with the craziest, busiest, hectic schedule I've ever had in my life. Why? Because I absolutely made self-care a priority. Without focusing on self, physically, emotionally, spiritually, and mentally, we are not giving ourselves the opportunity to grow. There is no way that you can effectively take on all the roles that you have without taking care of yourself. There's literally no way, and I completely understand that as a psychologist, as a human being, and as a productive citizen how important it is. So again, number one, I want you to make the commitment to self-care.

One example of a free thing to do for self-care is to consider spending more time in nature. There are many studies that show how taking a walk in nature and spending time outdoors is good for your mental health. It is free for you to watch a sunset or a sunrise, depending on who you are. I will tell you as an aside, I am not a morning person so normally I'm enjoying my sunsets instead of my sunrises (just saying). But nonetheless, it costs you $0 to engage in these activities, like watching sunrises or sunsets or taking a walk by a beach. If you're near a beach or taking a walk by a lake or river, a mountain, a park, or whatever type of outdoor places that you have around you, treat yourself and take in the beauty of nature.

Another thing I want you to remember about self-care is sometimes you need things to be solo, meaning you need to spend time doing self-care activities that bring you joy and that you are doing by yourself. One of the common questions that I get asked as a psychologist is, "What do you do for self-care, Dr. Hammond?" Well, I love being in nature as often as I can. I love to read. I love to workout really hard. I love to work on my mindset. I love my self-care books. I love any new form of wellness activity that is going to work on making me a better version of who I am. That is what I love, and that is why I'm dedicated to making sure that I'm doing these things. I'm making sure that I am the number one priority in my life so that I can show up in the best version of who I am for myself and those around me.

I want you to think for yourself right now. What is something you truly enjoy? Now you may say I don't have the time to add in any extra self-care. We can't create more than twenty-four hours in a day. We just can't; it's impossible. But what you can do is think about what you enjoy so much that would make you willing to change your schedule and priority list. Does it mean you have to watch one less Netflix show? Does it mean you have to give up something that you weren't really benefiting from anyway, so you can instead fill your time with something you enjoy? What solo activities come to mind that bring you joy?

When you think about the time commitment, ask yourself, how much time can you dedicate to improving your life? Do you have an extra sixty minutes a week? Do you want to dedicate one full day to yourself a month? Do you want to dedicate sixty seconds a day? There are all different types of ways you can structure your self-care time. Get into a practice of checking in with yourself emotionally and mentally.

Believe me, I get it. Life is hectic! I don't have a structured day/time each week for self-care because my schedule is so different week to week. But wherever I'm at, especially when I'm traveling throughout the country, whether it's different work assignments, a speaking engagement, or wherever I'm located, I'm always looking for ways to incorporate self-care to achieve peace of mind. I've trained my brain to look for ways to take care of myself by looking for ways to enjoy the lakes, mountains, sunsets, or any beautiful scenery around me.

It can be really easy for you to get caught up in all the negativity that is always surrounding you every single day. If you look at social media, traditional media, the news etc., you will often be viewing negative pictures, videos, and stories. Instead, when you devote a part of your self-care journey to working on changing your mindset and focusing on positivity, you can see the good that does exist and the beauty in nature. Sometimes all of the toxicity in the world makes you feel like the world is falling apart and ending. It feels like it, but the reality is there's still so much positivity in the world. There are still good people; there's still positivity.

What does that mean for your self-care? You find a way to train your brain. All of us are on a self-care journey. Some of you are at the starting line, and that's okay. Some of you are in the middle of a race, and that's okay. Because guess what, when this race is over, you're going to have another one to run. That's just how it works. This is a lifetime commitment that you should make when it comes to your self-care, which is critically important.

The other thing for you to recognize is that you have to start assessing some things when it comes to self-care. Ask yourself questions like: How am I doing? Do I need more time by myself right now? Or do I need time to be with friends and family? What is it that I am lacking? What is it that can motivate and inspire me, bringing me joy in this part of my life? For some of you, you absolutely need more time with yourself for self-care and for some of you, you need more time with friends and family, but only you can answer that. Ask yourself, what is it that you need in order to really think about the best self-care for you? A book that I really enjoyed, *Atomic Habits* by James Clear, discusses the idea of working to be better – one percent better per day. I want you to take this philosophy when it comes to your self-care if you're in a hard place right now.

Recap

- What amount of time can you devote to self-care: Once a week? Once a day? Once a month? What is realistic for you?
- Ask yourself: What brings me joy?
- Do a self-assessment often: How am I doing? Do I need more time by myself right now? Do I need time to be with friends and family? What is it that I am lacking? What is it that can motivate and inspire me, bringing me joy in this part of my life?

CHAPTER THREE
SELF-CARE IS NOT SELFISH

"Always grateful, never settle."

— JEREMY ANDERSON

YOU'VE PROBABLY HEARD THE SAYING BY NOW THAT SELF-CARE IS NOT selfish. For the past couple of years, I've loved hearing thoughts from people about self-care throughout the globe on my Livestream, *Mental Health Moment with Dr. Hammond* (it's on Black Women Empowered, Inc. FB, LinkedIn, and YouTube Live every Tuesday at 8 p.m. EST). I heard stories from literally around the world and every single continent, except for Antarctica (so fun!). One of the things that often comes up time after time from people of all different walks of life, from all over the continents, from all over the world, is this notion of whether self-care is selfish.

The problem is that we have to retrain our brains, because some of us grew up where there was this idea that if we took care of ourselves first, we're being selfish if we didn't put everyone, everything, and every responsibility above ourselves, that we were somehow not going to be successful. I remember, while growing up, that there was such a focus on achieving with this "go, go, go" attitude that there was no conversation about mental health or self-care or any conversation about how you should focus on you and put yourself first.

The reality is, it's actually the complete opposite of being selfish to take care of yourself. Because when you show up as the best version of who you are to those people around you, and when you show up with kindness and compassion, you are giving the best that you can. When you come from a place that is healed, a place that is strong emotionally, mentally, spiritually, financially, and physically, and you're uplifted and motivated, you can better help those around you. And then you're trying to help those people in your lives. And then you're trying to work, whether you're in school, whether it's your job, whether it's organizations you serve, volunteering, whatever it is that you're doing in your life, when you show up in that place, you're helping everyone else around you to the best of your true abilities.

The thought process used to be in order to be a great person, you have to put everyone else first. This is false. Right now, today, I want to challenge you to know this is a false notion that you need to put everyone else first. You are going to unlearn all the things that you have been taught that do not benefit your mental health. When it comes to your mental health, the fact is self-care is not selfish. These are not selfish things. Instead, spend your time investing in yourself, for you to work on the best version of who you are so you can show up as the best mom, dad, aunt, uncle, godparent, foster parent, significant other, sister, brother, coworker, corporate executive, entrepreneur, volunteer, whomever it is that you are for other people around you. You have to make sure you're taking care of yourself.

When I think about all the stories that I've heard, it usually entails somebody being a caregiver in some capacity for someone else. I've heard stories about people being caregivers of their parents, their children, and strong supporters of friends and neighbors and coworkers. One of the things that's so important to think about is how in the world do you juggle all these responsibilities? How do you juggle all these things, though, if you're not taking care of you, which is why it is critically important to ask yourself, "How do I need to put myself first?"

Imagine if you drew a triangle and wrote your name at the top of the triangle. Underneath your name can be your priorities and responsibilities in your life. Everything else in your life is below you. Why? Because that is how the best version of you trickles down into the people, the places, the responsibilities, and everything else around you. Who you show up as trickles down. So, start to place your well-being first. Because again, you are helping those people around you to work on you.

YOU

The rest of your priority list

Repeat these phrases often:

I deserve to be happy.
I deserve to be emotionally healthy.
I deserve to be spiritually, mentally, emotionally, and physically well.

When you realize the impact of your self-care and also recognize that this is not an overnight process, you will really start to realize that your life can change in miraculous and amazing ways. I am so excited for you to be reading this information. I am so excited for you to take that step. We are all at a different stage in our healing journey. But when you start to take the step, no matter where you're at in your life, you are building yourself up. This is why it's so important for you to have the self-care that you need to be the best version of who you are for you. No matter what anyone tells you, devote to building up who you are so that you can become the best version of who you are to show up for yourself and to show up for those around you.

Most people that I have met want to work on self-care, but also admit "it's hard."

There has been no one that I know of that has said, "Man, I really regret putting myself first. I really regret growth. I really regret who I am and the better version of who I am now." No one has said that ever

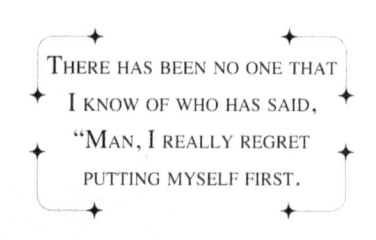

> THERE HAS BEEN NO ONE THAT I KNOW OF WHO HAS SAID, "MAN, I REALLY REGRET PUTTING MYSELF FIRST."

because growth can be a very positive thing. Does growth come with its challenges? Absolutely. But even in the process of evolving into a better state of mind, you can learn from those experiences. And if you need help with this process of changing your habits, a great book that I would highly recommend is *Atomic Habits* by

James Clear, which helps you organize your habits in small, doable steps.

Oftentimes we think about this; we think about our leaps and our bounds and these large goals, which there is nothing wrong with that, but it can be really frustrating sometimes when we make these giant goals and then we don't hit those goals in the time periods we set. Then we start to feel bad about ourselves, and those feelings may lead to depression and anxiety, and all these things happen. Instead, you can also take small, baby steps toward self-care because that absolutely counts too.

When it comes to your self-care journey, remember your **why.** A lot of times, I hear on *Mental Health Moment* that "it's hard to put myself first." It can be difficult to focus more on yourself, but there's different kinds of difficulties in this world. There's the kind of difficulty where you say this is so hard that it will never happen. That may be true, but with self-care, you can think of it as, "It's hard, but it'll take time because it's doable."

Let's try to reframe. It's hard, but it's doable. It's difficult, and it takes time. But it can be done. It's hard, but it's a challenge that I'm willing to accept. It's hard, but this could change my life. When I engage in a practice of putting myself first, it's hard, but I know I can do this. It's hard, but I can utilize my support systems around me to help me get through. It's hard, but I've made a commitment to this, and I'm going to stick through it. So, let's agree that it is hard, but also that it can be done.

Recap

- Self-care is NOT selfish.
- When you invest in being the best version of yourself, you can bring the best version of yourself to others in your life as well.
- Remember your why.

- Read or listen to *Atomic Habits* by James Clear.
- Repeat these phrases often:
- I deserve to be happy.
- I deserve to be emotionally healthy.
- I deserve to be financially, spiritually, mentally, emotionally, and physically well.

PART TWO
MENTAL SELF-CARE

"Strength doesn't just come from the body, it begins in the mind. Cultivate resilience, embrace challenges, and thrive mentally."

— DR. NEKESHIA HAMMOND

CHAPTER FOUR
POSITIVE SELF-TALK

"When you change your thoughts, remember to also change your world."

— NORMAL VINCENT PEALE

THERE ARE DIFFERENT TECHNIQUES TO HELP YOU WITH POSITIVE SELF-TALK. One of the most important things to think about when you're dealing with your thoughts is how to treat yourself with compassion. Many of us, as kids, were taught to treat others with kindness. We learned about the Golden Rule: Treat others as you would want to be treated. We learned all of these rules about how to treat other people. But one of the conversations that many of us never had growing up was how to treat ourselves and how important it is for us to treat ourselves with compassion, meaning how important it is for our thoughts to be positive. We have to think about how to address and understand the impact of those negative thoughts.

Your thoughts are very, very powerful. Read that last sentence again. When you think about your level of worthiness, you may have to adjust your self-talk. This is why you often see people using affirmations to train their brains how to work on positive self-talk. You may be thinking if I tell myself something positive that I don't believe anyway, I don't think all this positivity stuff will work. Well, you're absolutely right. When you tell yourself something so outlandish that you don't at all believe it, it's going to be really hard for your mind to comprehend and make that a part of who you are. So, you may have to take baby steps.

Maybe don't tell yourself you're the most amazing human being in the entire world. That might be a stretch to believe, but you could start with telling yourself that even though you make mistakes (you're human after all), you're still worthy of being happy. You're still worthy of good things happening to you. You're still worthy of having positive mental health. You're allowed to make mistakes, so give yourself grace and forgiveness.

You can train your brain to start thinking about questions like: What are some positive things that I can do? What works for me to think about becoming the best version of who I am when it comes to my positive self-talk? Is it affirmations? Is it different techniques that I need? And do I need to work on treating myself with more kindness?

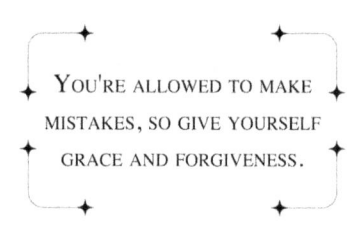

> YOU'RE ALLOWED TO MAKE MISTAKES, SO GIVE YOURSELF GRACE AND FORGIVENESS.

I want you to do a quick exercise. Think about the person that you love the most in this world. Imagine this person that you absolutely adore and love the most. Would you intentionally scream and yell vicious things to them and treat them with anger every single day with angry words? Probably not. That is why it's so important for you to understand if you wouldn't treat the person that you love the most like that every day intentionally, then you shouldn't be treating yourself like that either. But, many times what happens is we're so consumed with our negative thoughts and tell ourselves a lot of negative things that are not true. Those affirmations spiral into depression, anxiety, and other mental health concerns when we don't make a conscious effort of working on our positive self-talk.

Here are three easy strategies for you to implement to increase positive self-talk:

1. Become aware of your negative self-talk. This can be hard because studies show we have thousands and thousands of negative self-talk thoughts a day. So, you don't need to track every single one of your thoughts, but you need to work on being aware of what those thoughts are because a lot of times they show a pattern. It may be a pattern of you telling yourself you're not good enough. It may be you telling yourself you're not worthy. It may be you telling yourself you can't do something. It maybe you having conversations with yourself and blaming yourself for things that happened to you. There are many different types of negative self-talk, but when you get to the root of what you're saying to yourself, you can start to challenge those statements.
2. Replace those negative thoughts with positive thoughts. It's not easy. The thoughts are always going to be coming in, but you can challenge your thought process. You're allowed to go into battle. Go into battle in a good way. Show up and confront your own negative thoughts, telling yourself the negativity is not even true. Challenge your brain because most of the things you tell yourself are not even true anyway. You can challenge yourself to say these things aren't true and tell yourself what is true. ***What are the good things about you? What are your strengths? What are you good at?*** Write them down.
3. Don't blame yourself for how far you get in the journey of changing your self-talk because sometimes in our mental health journeys, we get frustrated with ourselves. It's okay to make a lot of progress and feel great but then see

the progress slow down. That's okay. Things happen. Just remember to take care of yourself and to trust the process.

Take a moment right now – like, right now - and write down five things you love about yourself. There's always something positive about you. There's always something good about you. Write those things down and read them periodically to remind yourself of who you are so you can show up as a powerful version of who you are. If you want to continue your transformative journey of self-discovery and positive self-talk, you can join my self-care masterclass at: mindsettrainingclass.com.

Recap

- Treat yourself with compassion.
- Your thoughts are very, very powerful.
- Three tips for positive self-talk:
- Become aware of your negative self-talk.
- Replace your negative thoughts with positive thoughts.
- Do not blame yourself during your journey.

CHAPTER FIVE
CLEARING YOUR MENTAL CLUTTER

"Keep your head clear. It doesn't matter how bright the path is if you head is always cloudy."

— UNKNOWN

THERE ARE MANY WAYS TO CLEAR MENTAL CLUTTER. MANY PEOPLE HAVE ideas swimming around in their heads; maybe ideas about what happened in their past, and maybe ideas about what's going on in their present, and maybe some thoughts and concerns about their future.

No matter what, you control your thoughts.

> NO MATTER WHAT, YOU CONTROL YOUR THOUGHTS.

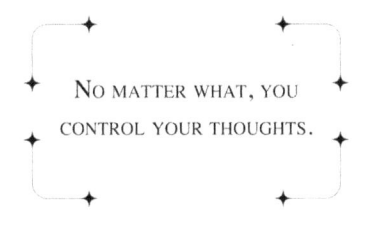

The book *Don't Believe Everything you Think* by Joseph Nguyen discusses this. It's a great reminder that you don't have to believe everything that you think because everything that you think is <u>not</u> true.

We get into this belief system, which is completely false, by the way, that if we think something in our heads, it must be true. We tell ourselves inaccurate and distorted and false things *all the time*. Because, let's face it, our emotions trigger our reactions, and our emotions sometimes distort reality. Now think about a time when you've been really angry with someone. Someone said something, and you may have taken it the wrong way and have been so angry about what they said. But when you came out of that angry state, you may have realized, "Wait a minute, that is not what they meant." And you recognized that your anger may have distorted the reality of the situation. This happens all of the time to all of us. It's important to recognize that your thoughts are not always reality. That being the case, you can work on decluttering your mind because a lot of thoughts might not be beneficial for you.

We all have different levels of negative self-talk, but the reality is that you can work on ways to declutter your mind. Here's an example - when you do what's called a brain dump, and you write things down and get it out of your head, those ideas that are churning may be a to-do list. Maybe you've been asking yourself why someone did something to you. Maybe you're asking yourself about your family members, or your friends or your worries; all sorts of things. It can be helpful to get those thoughts out of your head and write everything down as a brain dump. You can either jot it all down, write it down, or if you don't like writing, you can say it out loud. If you're in a car by yourself, or in any place, frankly, by yourself, say it out loud and get it out of your mind temporarily.

Use journaling and write your feelings out. Use silent time or meditation to work on your body, getting into a calm place so you can get into a mode to get these feelings, emotions, the to-do list agitation, the frustrations, all those things out. Talk to a trusted friend. Utilize different methods to get out your feelings because it's all a part of your process to clear out your mental clutter, which goes back to the mental health detox, discussed in a later chapter in this book.

Work on clearing out the mental clutter to work on reducing distress. Will it cure depression or anxiety? Will it magically make these situations go away in your life that are stressful? Of course not. But when you think of a healthy way to deal with your stress, as opposed to unhealthy ways, a brain dump can be one of those things that can help you clear your mental clutter.

Just as with a place, when you think about clearing out the clutter in your closet or in your office or home ,or wherever it is that you have physical clutter, sometimes the clutter returns. It's the same way with your mental clutter. You will always be in states in life where you will go from having a low stress day to having what you feel is the most stressful day of your life. This is the reality of life. In my first book, *The Practical Guide to Raising Emotionally Healthy Children*, I talked about the idea that if children had an opportunity to learn how to manage their emotions early, it is a complete gift to them when they move into their adult years, because mismanagement of emotions is the reason for many insecurities, complexes, bad relationships, and conflicts.

Emotional dysregulation can lead to difficulties in relationships. Emotional distress and burnout can lead to problems in the workplace. These are the reasons for problems in friendships and family life such as, substance abuse, depression, and anxiety, much of it stemming from difficulties managing emotions. I've met many people who have been terminated from their jobs because of difficulties managing their emotions.

You're most likely an adult as you read this book, but I want you to understand that it's never too late to work on clearing your own mental clutter and making it a habit like, how you might clear out your desktop, some apps on your phone, or physical places in your home. Your mind is one of the most powerful environments that you are around 24/7.

Your thoughts are incredibly powerful.

> **YOUR THOUGHTS ARE INCREDIBLY POWERFUL. USE THEM WISELY.**

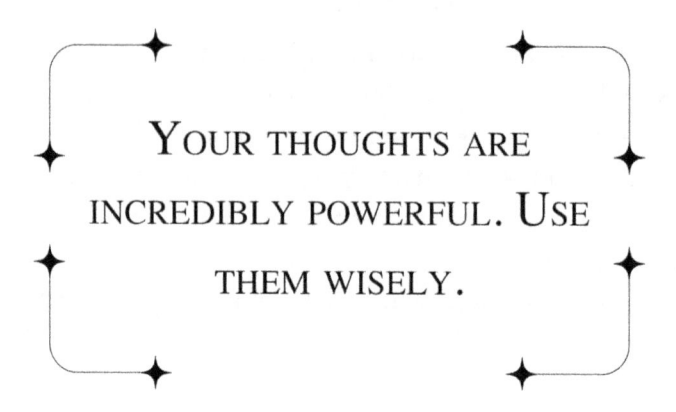

Use them wisely. What you work on within your mental wellness journey is critical for your well-being, which is why it's so important to work on having a strategy that you commit to in clearing out your mental clutter.

Recap

- Check out the book, *Don't Believe Everything You Think*, by Joseph Nguyen.
- Practice doing a "brain dump" to clear your mental clutter.
- Just like physical clutter, mental clutter often returns, so make it a practice to clear your mental clutter periodically.

CHAPTER SIX

MINDSET TRAINING

"An eagle uses the storm to reach unimaginable heights."

— ET THE HIP HOP PREACHER

ONE OF THE IDEAS THAT YOU'VE PROBABLY HEARD ABOUT IS THIS NOTION OF mental toughness. When it comes to elite athletes, we've often heard stories of intense physical training and incredible accomplishments within a sport. These athletes are working on being very high performers when it comes to athletics, but we all know for the best athletes, they don't just focus on physical training, they focus on mental training as well. Mental training is paramount for success. It's a mindset shift that needs to happen to work on being the best athlete and outshine the competition.

The good news is you don't have to be an elite athlete to work on your mindset training, it's for everyone. Your mental toughness, your ability to be resilient, your ability to work on being the best version of who you are, is something that should be set aside. In this chapter, I'm going to teach you how to work on your own mindset training.

The first thing to think about is your ability to withstand and endure life's disappointments, challenges, and struggles. No matter who you are on the planet, life will always throw you a curveball. It isn't rocket science to know that life has its ups and downs. But it's all about how you manage your emotions and how you train your brain to be able to handle everything – good or bad – life can throw at you.

There are people in this world who you might consider to be a "strong person." Think about those people that you know around you; maybe you are who everyone thinks is the "strong" one. That's okay. You're absolutely positively allowed to be a strong, amazing person. But you also have to have the mindset to understand that you are going to have to deal with so many things, unanticipated events that you will have to train your brain to handle. One of the things I have learned in talking with thousands and thousands of people all throughout the country, and at different places in the world, is that *you are stronger than you think*. You have been able to handle so many things that have happened to you in your life.

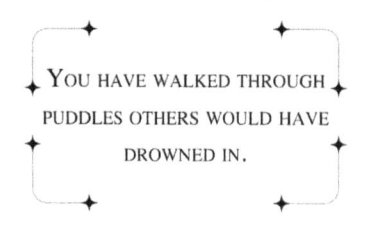

> YOU HAVE WALKED THROUGH PUDDLES OTHERS WOULD HAVE DROWNED IN.

You have walked through puddles others would have drowned in.

Mindset training is finding the answers to what you need to do on a daily, weekly, or monthly basis and incorporating them consistently.

In my work with kids, many times, bullying comes up. Especially for my little ones that I've had conversations with, it is literally a conversation of, "What do you say back to this person? How do you respond in anticipation of this person?" They are at a loss on how to handle emotions of inferiority, rage, fear, and feeling less than. Should they punch back, kick, hit, or do something harmful to the other individual? All valid responses, most would think. However, it goes deeper than lashing back out. I teach my kids on how to develop a mental armor, if you will.

When we think about a knight in shining armor, we think about the protection of this knight in case there is a battle. However there's also a mental armor that can protect us in difficult situations. I want you to think about how are you developing your own mental armor? This doesn't just work for kids, developing mental armor is helpful for adults as well. And no, it's not about you not experiencing or suppressing your feelings or emotions. It's not about blocking everything out. You should absolutely feel emotions, as you're ready to process the things that are happening to you. But it is also about not allowing certain situations to be so harmful to you mentally that you cannot function.

Now, I know what you may be thinking, *But Dr. Hammond, there are situations that are so profoundly difficult. It feels like I'm breaking down; it feels like I can't get out of bed, it feels like I'm so anxious, etc.* It may feel like some days that you cannot function because you wonder if you'll be in situations that bring you to negative, debilitating feelings. I get it, seek professional help. I don't want to minimize how important it is reach out to a mental health professional when necessary.

It's important for you to be doing the intervention that you need to do to move through those times and those spaces in the way that works best for you. But in the same token, it's also important to recognize that there are preventative measures you can take to work on your mindset so that you can have more resilience to certain situations.

Now, are there certain situations that are just more difficult to deal with than others? Absolutely. I have complete empathy and compassion for many different situations. Hearing stories of PTSD, social anxiety, ADHD, learning issues, depression, burnout, and the list goes on and on. It's hard. I totally understand that. This chapter is not about you working on a way to not feel anything, but instead, it's working on a way for you, despite the obstacles, to do the best you can. So, when that situation arises, you can do the best that you can to cope and move through the difficult times that will come up.

One of the incredibly hard and challenging things for me in 2020 was the loss of my very close mentor, Yusuf Salaam. I actually dedicated this book to him because he was such an inspirational force in my life. I had the pleasure of being mentored by him for the last five years of his life. It rocked me to my core to get a phone call in July 2020 that he had lost his life unexpectedly.

I can't express in this book the difficulty with grief and how I literally thought I would run out of tears to cry. It was so emotionally painful and difficult for a long time. But one of the things that helped get me through that time was my faith, all the mindset training that I worked on, all of the inner work, if you will, that I had done for years and years before that. I really honestly believe that all of those things helped to prepare me to deal with that level of grief to the best of my abilities. I'm not saying it was easy; there's still some days that are hard, but it was possible to cope and get through the pain.

Building up your resiliency can help to prepare you to deal with situations in a more effective manner. So, I encourage you to start today and think about what you need to do to work on your mindset to be stronger, to grow stronger, to have the mental toughness, to have the ability to get through, to have the mindset that you can handle most of what life throws at you. However, if you're in a situation where you're having some really difficult times of doing this on your own, which is okay, please reach out to a mental health professional to make sure your needs are taken care of as you work through this journey of mindset training.

Recap

- You are stronger than you think.
- Mindset training is powerful in preparing you for life's challenges.
- Ask yourself: which mindset training tool will I add into my life today?

CHAPTER SEVEN
INNER PEACE

"The more you praise and celebrate your life, the more there is in life to celebrate."

— OPRAH WINFREY

ONE OF THE THINGS YOU CAN DO WHEN YOU THINK ABOUT YOUR INNER PEACE is think about what you can celebrate. Find a reason to celebrate. I know what you're thinking. This is probably really difficult to do, especially when you're in a hard place in life. But when you learn how to find the smallest thing even to celebrate, it can make some of the difficult times a bit more manageable. So, one of the things to think about is how can you celebrate any small thing that is meaningful to you? Even in the midst of your dark times, even in the midst of feeling sad, even in the midst of feeling anxious, even in the midst of loneliness, even in the midst of transition, how can you celebrate?

One practical way that you can celebrate is to do something that brings you joy, whether it be something that takes a full day, an hour, a few minutes, or whatever timeframe you want. Oftentimes, what happens is, by society's measures, we are encouraged to celebrate the times that are on a calendar. Like maybe if you celebrate Christmas or if you celebrate birthdays, or if you celebrate anniversaries, or whatever it is, that is "supposed to" be celebrated at a particular time, but that doesn't mean all the other days in the year that you can't celebrate something, right? So, what you want to think about is how you can add days to your calendar, and it doesn't have to even be something you do every year.

One of the things that was pretty fun that we've done for a while with my child is celebrate half- birthdays. So, it's not a huge celebration where we get friends and family together, but it might just be a quick, "Hey, we're thinking about you, and we're celebrating that we love you with a cupcake," just a simple cupcake. Giving an extra hug that day or doing something that makes a child feel special goes a long way.

I like to find any reason to celebrate. It could be just having a great day as something to celebrate. It could be hitting a goal that you have; it could be the fact that you got through something really difficult you didn't think you were going to get through. In what way you celebrate depends on you.

You may celebrate by going out to eat, which is a pretty common way to celebrate. We oftentimes think about how we celebrate by going out to eat with friends or family members, or you can take yourself on a date. A self-date can be out to eat, alone to a movie, enjoying your favorite desert and book, shopping for a particular item you've long wanted, a smoothie after the gym, and anything you've wanted to do for a while but haven't made the time.

Think about other ways to celebrate, like maybe getting your nails done or a massage or having some type of calming experience for yourself, such as not taking business calls for a day, getting a massage, going to the beach, listen to live music, spending more time in prayer, talking a leisurely walk through a park, or anything that calms your nerves. When it comes to celebration, you can do it by yourself or with loved ones. You get to decide what this looks like.

I want to empower you to think about the question: "How can I create more joy and inner peace in my life?" Really think about the question.

One of the ways to create more joy is to think about how you celebrate, so make sure you are scheduling in time for yourself. I'm listing some different options to celebrate, but this is by no means an exhaustive list. You can choose to add all of these to your calendar, or you could choose to add which ones work for you. So, here's a quick list of some examples of ways that you can celebrate:

- Celebrate a half-birthday.
- Enjoy a cup of tea.
- Take yourself on a date.
- Enjoy a glass of wine.
- Celebrate with your favorite meal.
- Go for a walk.
- Get a massage.
- Decide to have a calming day.
- Go fishing.
- Carve out thirty minutes of me time.
- Schedule a rest and relaxation weekend.
- Do your favorite hobby.
- Spend time with your loved ones.
- Hang out with your pet.
- Spend time in nature.
- Take a road trip.
- Garden.
- Buy yourself flowers.
- Light a scented candle.
- Watch your favorite movie.
- Travel to a new place.

You have to decide on how celebration looks and works for you, and also decide about which ones apply, which ones are feasible, and which ones bring you the most joy. In another part of this book, we'll discuss what feelings you want to experience because a lot of times, our sadness or anxiety or overall distress is because we are not experiencing what we want to be feeling. What is it for you that you want to experience more of? Do you want to experience more calmness? Do you want to experience more happiness or peace of mind or joy?

You should often be in this conversation with yourself to understand what it is that you want.

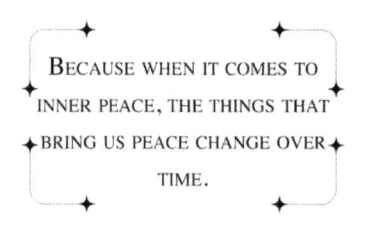

> Because when it comes to inner peace, the things that bring us peace change over time.

Because when it comes to inner peace, the things that bring us peace change over time.

So, what may have brought you inner peace in your younger years may be completely different now. Whatever stage of life you're in, what feelings you want to experience is something else to keep in mind.

Working on your journey of inner peace and happiness is one way to connect with yourself. Increase your self-awareness and work on the next steps for you to regain inner peace. The other part of inner peace is what to do when the bumps in the road come along? Because that's what life is. There are certain tools that will get you into a place of inner peace. It can be deep breathing, meditation ,taking a walk in nature, spending time with people who are good for your mental health, or having a good laugh. There are many ways to get into a state of inner peace. Sometimes there's something that's going to come along in your life that is going to completely disrupt your inner peace. Don't panic – it's called life.

When you are aware of what you can do to get back into a place of inner peace, that is when you are truly in a powerful place to move through this thing called life.

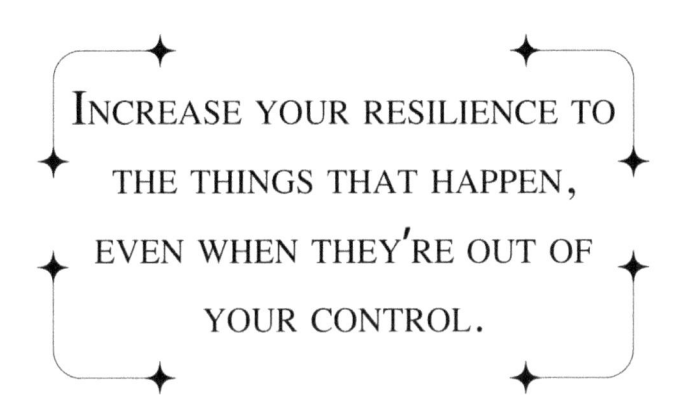

> **INCREASE YOUR RESILIENCE TO THE THINGS THAT HAPPEN, EVEN WHEN THEY'RE OUT OF YOUR CONTROL.**

Increase your resilience to the things that happen, even when they're out of your control.

Still feel the feelings that come along, but also work on processing through that difficult time and moving back into a state of inner peace. You can do this.

Recap

- Schedule in celebrations often.
- What *feels* do you want to experience more of? Calmness? Peace of mind? Happiness?
- Commit to building your resilience to handle the ebb and flow of life.

CHAPTER EIGHT
PERMISSION TO HEAL

> "The dark does not destroy the light; it defines it. It's our fear of the dark that casts our joy into the shadows."
>
> — BRENÉ BROWN

THIS NOTION OF GIVING YOURSELF PERMISSION IS EXTREMELY IMPORTANT FOR you to recognize. You have to give yourself permission to heal from whatever life brought to you in the past, is bringing you in the present, or will bring you in the future. It starts with you giving yourself permission to heal from the challenges of life, the disappointments of life, the hard times of life, the surprises of life, the way it should have been, could have been, and would have been. **Give yourself full permission to heal.**

Allow yourself to remember that you deserve to be happy.

You deserve to have a full, happy, abundant life. You deserve to experience positivity. You deserve to be around people who uplift you. You deserve to have positive content around you.

> ✦ ALLOW YOURSELF TO REMEMBER THAT YOU DESERVE TO BE HAPPY. ✦

You can be an inspirational story no matter what your background is or what people in society have told you that you're supposed to be. That is something personally that I have dealt with my whole life, people judging me based on knowing absolutely *nothing* about me. Simply because of the way I look, because of my personality, because of what people project on me based on what's happening in their own lives, because of what society has told them someone like me was supposed to be ... all of those things. It is a constant reminder for me to work on not only being the best version of who I am, but also recognizing that we may think we don't deserve healing, or we may think that we're unworthy of it, but it's absolutely not true. **You deserve to be healed.** You deserve whatever it is best for you. You deserve your beautiful transformation.

For some of you, give yourself permission to go to therapy. For some of you, give yourself permission to experience joyful moments. For some of you, give yourself permission to take a day off. For some of you, give yourself permission to go into silent moments to take a minute to reset and recharge. For some of you, give yourself permission to forgive yourself for whatever it is you did, or whatever it is that you didn't do, or whatever it is that you were supposed to do, for whatever it is you could have done, you should have done, and all the things that you are blaming yourself for that you cannot turn back the hands of time and change. You deserve to have self-forgiveness. You can give yourself permission to start that journey or to continue that journey.

Once you finish the journey of self-forgiveness and have that peace of mind about whatever situation you're experiencing, you can give yourself permission to get through whatever it was that hurt you, even those done by someone you cared about.

And just as how you have to give yourself permission to start any project, any goal, any new ideas, you have to give yourself permission to continue this journey of your mental health and wellness. If you said that you wanted to lose twenty pounds, give yourself permission to start that journey.

Maybe you want to try a new exercise routine. Maybe you want to work with a personal trainer, or you want to go to the gym more often because you've already given yourself permission to change and to lose weight, and you've committed to reaching your weight-loss goals. Well, in the same manner when it comes to healing yourself and when it comes to being a better version of you, you have to give yourself permission to start this journey, knowing that you will absolutely be confronted with challenges you didn't expect. It's the same exact thing with the weight-loss journey. There's always going to be challenges. Are you prepared to handle those challenges? Are you prepared for them emotionally?

Have you set yourself up with mental armor? You can be your knight, your own knight in shining armor, with the mental armor you are building up with yourself so you can handle life's challenges as best as you can. It doesn't make you a perfect person. If you said, "Today, I give myself permission to heal," this proclamation by no means makes you a perfect person who is not susceptible to experiencing depression or anxiety or loss or trauma or grief. But what it does is it gives yourself permission to think about how you can work on being a stronger person. Think about this: *How can I heal from the things I need to heal from while also recognizing that I'm a human being and am allowed to have those feelings?*

We often hear about the person who has to be strong. "You just have to be strong," society says. You just have to get through and cope with all these things that are thrown at you. Or we have this idea of another type of person who cannot manage what's happening to them, and we think of this extreme spectrum, *who's the strongest and who's the weakest?* Yet, the reality is you don't have to be at either end of the spectrum. You're allowed to give yourself permission to heal from the things that happen to you.

At some points in your life, be the strongest person mentally that you can be, but know that at other points in life, when you're dealing with something, you're allowed to have feelings about it and process these thing and still thrive as much as you can. There's this idea that every day we must be thriving, which is so unrealistic. Giving yourself permission to heal means you also have permission to take days off. I remember I was interviewed once by a media source about whether or not children should have mental health days. And I felt like screaming from the rooftops, "Yes!!" Personally, and professionally, as a mom, a psychologist, and a human being, when I was asked should kids be allowed to take a day off to reset, recharge, and deal with their anxiety and their depression and their concerns and their stresses, it seemed like a no-brainer to me. Absolutely! Our youth should have that ability to heal too.

We had perfect attendance awards at my school. And I still remember to this day, even though I was in elementary school quite a long time ago, how obsessed I was at getting this Perfect Attendance Award. I could not miss school regardless of the circumstances. I never wanted to miss, and, as noble as we think that is, what that does is it trains the minds of kids to think about not ever taking a day off for yourself. There are people, maybe you know some of these people, who work for twenty, thirty, forty years and are proud to say they've never taken a day off work or took a vacation. That saddens me so much. Because the reality is we all need a day off, and we all need some type of reset and recharge. How much time we need a year varies by each individual. There's no one-size-fits-all with this.

Not understanding the importance of taking that time off to reset and recharge is a common phenomenon though. More than likely, the person who worked twenty, thirty, or forty+ years had something happen in their lives where they needed healing. There might have been a loss, some type of grief, a negative change in a relationship, or maybe financial difficulties. Something bad happened but they believed they had to keep plowing on as if they had no feelings associated with it. It's mind-blowing because that type of behavior is very unhealthy.

And then we wonder when people do that, and they take no time off. They take no vacation time (and this is even with companies who would have paid for their vacations so they wouldn't have affected them). Man, it was the mentality of "Don't skip a day, don't take a day off." I was in that situation though as a child. I was in that situation where I would do anything that made sure I didn't miss a day of school. I never skipped school a day in my life. Heaven forbid I miss school. Geez! I had that type of unhealthy mindset. I thought that somehow, someway, if I missed a day or two of school it was going to ruin the rest of my life. Don't get me wrong; I'm all about education. But I'm also about making sure our kids are emotionally healthy too!

For most people, taking a day or two or three off work to reset can be refreshing and invigorating. I'm seeing more and more companies looking at this four-day workweek idea of really changing the environment of the workplace because of understanding now, "Hey, wait a minute, people's brains need a break. Right?" The goal of companies should be to embrace policies that prevent burnout for employees. In fact, burnout prevention can lead to higher productivity, increased retention rates, improved engagement in tasks, and more. After seeing more and more issues in work environments, I've started speaking more to groups about burnout prevention and as I write this book, I'm in conversations with Fortune 500 companies to start to implement my burnout prevention model for companies. I'm excited to be servicing in this space because the need for mental wellness is so great.

So going back to this notion of permission to heal, you work on giving yourself permission that you need to heal, that you need to heal and doing what you need to do to be the best version of who you are. This is what this entire book has been about you, when you become the best version of who you are. You're showing up for yourself, and you're showing up for everyone around you. This is not just about you; it's actually the complete opposite. When you give yourself that permission to heal, not only are you healing for you, but you're going to heal and help other people around you because you're in a more nurturing place.

Will something else pop up? Will something else happen? Will something else disrupt your inner peace? Absolutely. Hello, Life. Yes, it will. But then you go back to your process because you know the best way that you can work on healing. And that's when you really start to think about becoming the best version of who you can be. And think about your healing journey, about having a better quality of life that you deserve. Give yourself the permission you deserve to heal.

Recap

- You deserve to have healing.
- Consider when you need to reset and recharge your life.
- You're allowed to take a day off.
- Check out Jay Shetty's book *Think Like a Monk: Train Your Mind for Peace and Purpose Every Day*.

PART THREE
PHYSICAL SELF-CARE

"Every small step towards healing is a giant leap toward a brighter future."

— DR. NEKESHIA HAMMOND

CHAPTER NINE
NUTRITION, MOVEMENT, AND SLEEP

> "If you restore balance in your own self, you will be contributing immensely to the healing of the world."
>
> — DEEPAK CHOPRA

FROM THE BEGINNING OF TIME, IT FEELS LIKE THERE WAS ALWAYS A FOCUS ON physical health. There was always a focus on medicine for physical health and mental health really didn't get the recognition that it fully deserved until much later. But the good news is, there have been many studies that show the benefits of the mind-body connection. There are many benefits to working on your physical health which can affect your mental health and working on your mental health, which can affect your physical health.

NUTRITION

Your eating habits are important when it comes to mental health. What tends to happen is we feel bogged down, distressed, and maybe even depressed and anxious and with attention issues because our diet is so poor. I am not here to say that certain diets are *curing* any mental health conditions.

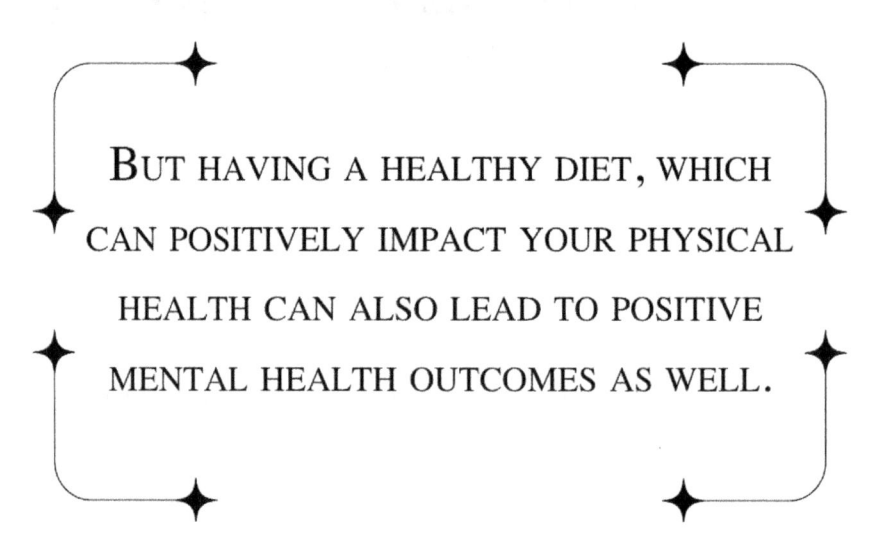

> **BUT HAVING A HEALTHY DIET, WHICH CAN POSITIVELY IMPACT YOUR PHYSICAL HEALTH CAN ALSO LEAD TO POSITIVE MENTAL HEALTH OUTCOMES AS WELL.**

But having a healthy diet, which can positively impact your physical health can also lead to positive mental health outcomes as well.

So really take an assessment of what you're eating and how you can improve your diet to improve your physical health.

Dr. Eva Selhub in a Harvard Health blog entitled "Nutritional psychiatry: Your brain on food", talks about the importance of nutrition for your mental health. She noted, "Studies have compared "traditional" diets, like the Mediterranean diet and the traditional Japanese diet, to a typical "Western" diet and have shown that the risk of depression is 25% to 35% lower in those who eat a traditional diet. Scientists account for this difference because these traditional diets tend to be high in vegetables, fruits, unprocessed grains, and fish and seafood, and to contain only modest amounts of lean meats and dairy..." This among other research illustrate the power of a good diet for positive mental health outcomes.

Nutrition plays a pivotal role in mental health, and making intentional changes to your diet can have profound effects on cognitive function and emotional well-being. Incorporating a variety of nutrient-dense foods, including fruits, vegetables, whole grains, lean proteins, and healthy fats, provides the essential vitamins and minerals needed for optimal brain function. Omega-3 fatty acids found in fatty fish, flaxseeds, and walnuts, for instance, have been linked to improved mood and cognitive performance. By prioritizing a well-balanced and diverse diet, you can ensure a steady supply of nutrients that support neurotransmitter production and regulate your mood.

Reducing the intake of processed foods, sugary snacks, and excessive caffeine is another crucial step toward enhancing mental health through nutrition. Refined sugars and highly processed foods can lead to fluctuations in blood sugar levels, affecting energy levels and mood. Opting for whole, unprocessed foods helps maintain stable blood sugar, providing a consistent and sustained source of energy for the brain. Furthermore, staying hydrated by drinking an adequate amount of water throughout the day is essential, as dehydration can impair cognitive function and contribute to feelings of fatigue and irritability.

MOVEMENT

Imagine working on your mental health and working on the calming techniques you can utilize in mindset training. You can work and understand there's a huge mind-body connection that allows you to have a better prognosis with physical health conditions. The other part to recognize is sometimes you can be engaged in activities that can help you both physically and mentally, take for instance, different forms of exercise.

Many studies show that depression can be alleviated by exercise. The physical benefits of exercise also extend into your mental health as well. When we look at the benefits of exercise, we understand that physical activity can helps with your heart health, blood pressure, diabetes, weight management, and various other conditions.

There are also benefits on the mental health side that these forms of physical exercise can help with, like reducing anxiety, reducing depression, helping with better concentration, improving sleep, all these sorts of issues that come about because sometimes your mental stresses can really get stuck in your physical body. The stress that you have mentally can start to weigh down your physical body and affect you in different ways if it's not addressed, but the good news is there's a lot of different ways to engage in physical exercise.

For example, you may not like running but like to bike or walk. One of the misconceptions that I have learned in my conversations with many people that don't exercise is they think that exercise has to look a certain way. Here's the reality. It's better for you to exercise in a way that you love than to not exercise at all (just make sure it's approved by your physician).

A strong correlation exists between physical health and positive mental well-being, as regular movement activities contribute to a cascade of benefits for the mind. Cardiovascular exercises, such as brisk walking or jogging, stimulate the release of endorphins – the body's natural mood elevators. These feel-good chemicals not only help alleviate stress and anxiety but also contribute to an overall sense of happiness and well-being. Engaging in group fitness classes further amplifies these benefits by fostering a social connection, reducing feelings of isolation, and promoting a sense of community, all of which are vital elements for positive mental health.

Additionally, movement activities that focus on flexibility and balance, like yoga or Pilates, have been shown to have a profound impact on mental health. These practices emphasize mindfulness, deep breathing, and meditation, promoting relaxation and stress reduction. Improved posture and body awareness achieved through these activities also contribute to a positive self-image and increased self-esteem. Outdoor activities, such as hiking or participating in recreational sports, offer an opportunity to connect with nature, which has been linked to reduced levels of depression and increased feelings of well-being. In essence, the holistic approach to physical health not only nurtures the body but also acts as a powerful catalyst for cultivating a positive and resilient mental state.

Just start! Make sure you seek physician approval for any exercise regimens that you're going to begin and do know that there's so many benefits of physical activity and improving your mental health. You can also find a great article, "The Mental Health Benefits of Exercise" at helpguide.org with additional information about exercise and the positive impact on your mental wellness.

SLEEP

According to Health.gov, "Most adults need 7 or more hours of good-quality sleep on a regular schedule each night." We live in a world that focuses so much on being busy and sometimes neglecting our own sleep, but sleep is critical to your health. I've met many people who struggle with sleeping, which is associated with depression, anxiety, burnout, and other mental and emotional health issues. What I often hear is, "I can't turn my brain off," or "My mind keeps racing at night." Health.gov goes on to list the common signs of sleep disorders, which may include:

- Trouble falling or staying asleep
- Still feeling tired after a good night's sleep
- Sleepiness during the day that makes it difficult to do everyday activities, like driving or concentrating at work
- Frequent loud snoring
- Pauses in breathing or gasping while sleeping
- Tingling or crawling feelings in your legs or arms at night that feel better when you move or massage the area

- Feeling like it's hard to move when you first wake up

Establishing healthy sleep habits is crucial for your overall well-being, as quality sleep is closely linked to mental health. One key habit is maintaining a consistent sleep schedule by going to bed and waking up at the same time every day, even on weekends. This helps regulate the body's internal clock, promoting a more restful and uninterrupted sleep. Creating a calming bedtime routine, such as reading a book, taking a warm bath, or practicing relaxation techniques like deep breathing, signals to the body that it's time to wind down. Additionally, ensuring a comfortable sleep environment, with a cool and dark room, supportive mattress, and minimal disruptions, fosters an atmosphere conducive to restorative sleep.

The relationship between sleep and mental health is bidirectional, with each influencing the other. Adequate and quality sleep is essential for cognitive function, emotional regulation, and stress resilience. During sleep, the brain consolidates memories, processes emotions, and removes toxins accumulated throughout the day. Chronic sleep deprivation, on the other hand, is associated with an increased risk of mood disorders, anxiety, and impaired decision-making. By prioritizing good sleep hygiene, you can promote mental health by enhancing cognitive functioning, emotional well-being, and overall resilience to life's challenges. Cultivating healthy sleep habits is a proactive and effective approach to supporting your mental health.

If you are concerned about your sleep, it's important that you reach out to a physician to follow up and assess next best steps. Sleep problems can stem from physical and/or emotional/mental health issues, so make sure you reach out for support. You can also find a link to a "Your guide to healthy sleep" published by the U.S. Health & Human Services in the "Resources" section.

Recap:
Physical

- Start with small, mindful changes in your nutrition habits
- Remember that good nutrition can have a significant positive impact on mental well-being
- Focus on nutrient-rich foods and reduce processed foods

Movement

- Understand the mind-body connection can have incredible benefits for you
- Engage in forms of exercise that you enjoy (and are approved by your physician)
- Ask yourself: In what way do I need to improve my physical health? Is it through sleep, diet, exercise, or something else?

Sleep

- Make healthy sleep habits a top priority
- Reach out to a physician if you are concerned about your sleep
- Ask yourself: What steps do I need to take to improve my sleep?

PART FOUR
EMOTIONAL SELF-CARE

"Today's challenges are tomorrow's victories. Embrace each moment with courage and hope."

— DR. NEKESHIA HAMMOND

CHAPTER TEN
MINDFULNESS PRACTICES

> "Success isn't always about greatness. It's about consistency. Consistent hard work leads to success. Greatness will come".
>
> — DWAYNE JOHNSON

THERE ARE MANY THINGS YOU CAN DO FOR MINDFULNESS. MINDFULNESS IS A concept that means taking the time to refocus and be and live in the present moment. For many of us, it is very common to be worrying about the past or thinking about the future, having anxiety about what's to come or having sadness about what should have happened or could have happened or did not happen. That's a very common feeling. But the reality is it's a very peaceful place when you think about trying to live more in the present moment. One of my favorite books, *The Power of Now* by Eckhart Tolle, talks about how peaceful it can be when you take moments of time to consciously live in the present moment.

What can mindfulness look like? It can look like paying very close attention to what is happening around you. Now, I know what you may be thinking. You don't have enough time. You don't have enough energy. It's so exhausting. You might be inundated with messages about this "mindfulness" thing and these mindfulness techniques that you probably have heard or seen about on social media or heard from a friend. But here's the thing: with mindfulness training, you can start with what you're already doing.

Look at your current routine. For most of you, you have a steady routine every day. It may include something like, for example, washing your face in the morning, brushing your teeth, taking a shower. Getting ready for your day. As you're doing those things, I want you to really concentrate on the action of doing that task. For example, if you brushed your teeth in the morning, you could think about putting the toothpaste on the toothbrush, turning on the water, putting the toothpaste and toothbrush under the running water, then putting the toothbrush in your mouth, brushing your teeth, then taking the toothbrush out of your mouth, rinsing the toothbrush off, turning the water off, and putting your toothbrush away.

The reason why I gave you all those steps is because that's literally what your mind has to be focusing on. It's a short amount of time, but it's something I have utilized as well when I was starting my own mindfulness training to really be present in the moment, because a lot of times when we're brushing our teeth, or we're in the shower, or we're driving or whatever it is we're doing, we're thinking about something else besides the present moment. And what happens is you've completely missed the beauty of life. This is also why I love to spend a lot of time in nature. I love being in the beautifulness of nature, the calmness of trees and serenity that mountains, rivers, and beaches can bring to your day. Sometimes spending time in nature can make it seem like time can stand still, if only for a short, peaceful moment.

Your goal with mindfulness training is to get yourself into a calmer, peaceful state of mind. Now, is this calming state going to erase your problems in life? Of course not. I've always said I wish I had a magic wand to just magically help people and make them feel better, but I haven't gotten that wish granted yet. I have wanted that since I was a kid, but as we know, there is no magic wand that instantly makes problems go away.

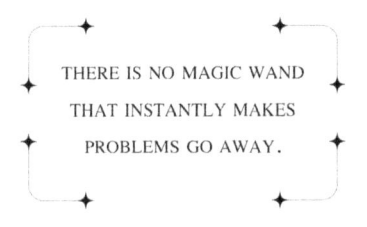

> THERE IS NO MAGIC WAND THAT INSTANTLY MAKES PROBLEMS GO AWAY.

But instead, when you work on getting into calming spaces, being in the present moment, you start to train your brain to accept that you are allowed to have those peaceful times. You're allowed to have those joyous moments, and you're allowed to have calmness and peace in your life, even when the rest of your day may be really hectic.

I have a hashtag that I love using called #takeaminute. I've loved to find sixty seconds out of my day (at a minimum) to really focus on the present moment. In those sixty seconds, you get to decide what you do in those sixty seconds. Some examples are: You can take deep breaths. You can pray if you believe in prayer. You can go into complete silence. You can listen to some calming music. You can take a minute to think about all the good things that are happening to you in your life. Or you could take sixty seconds to just relax and have a cup of coffee, cup of tea, or whatever it is that is calming for you. Why sixty seconds? We all have ONE minute that we can devote to ourselves, right? There are so many demands on our time and energy on a daily basis.

Back in 2020, when the COVID-19 pandemic became very real here in the U.S. and globally, one of the things I found to be the most calming when we were quarantined in our house was to just take a cup of tea, a simple cup of tea, have a seat on the couch, and just focus on drinking my tea and taking some deep breaths. It was a very stressful time. I had to shut down my private practice temporarily at the time. I had my son at home full-time because we were doing virtual school, of course, because school was closed, while trying to make sense of a global pandemic with my then seven-year-old son. I was also dealing that summer, July 2020, with heavy grief from losing a very close mentor.

Throughout those months of dealing with this pandemic, while trying to navigate ways to be safe, trying to keep my family safe, trying to explain what was happening to this young child of mine at home, dealing with the murder of George Floyd, and having to explain that and everything that was happening in the world to my son, it was heavy. Very heavy.

Another mindfulness technique that can work on managing stress is called the 5-4-3-2-1 technique, where you stop and focus on:

5 things you can <u>see.</u>
4 things you can <u>hear.</u>
3 things you can <u>touch.</u>
2 things you can <u>smell.</u>
1 thing you can <u>taste.</u>

With this technique, you can practice grounding yourself, focus on your senses, and be present in the moment.

There will be very heavy times in your life. There will, also, be very happy times in your life. We all have a different season that we're in. But the good news is that you can give your brain a break and find those mindfulness moments to take a minute and think about how you can really take the time to work on you. Plus, mindfulness strategies have really been shown to help you physically, emotionally, mentally, and spiritually. There are a lot of benefits to mindfulness training. I hope that you will incorporate some mindfulness strategies to really work on seeing yourself thrive as an individual.

Recap

- Mindfulness can start by taking one daily task (like brushing your teeth) and focusing on the present moment while doing this task.
- Find sixty seconds (at a min.) in each day to focus on the present.
- Ask yourself: Why is mindfulness important to me? How can I take a minute each day to practice mindfulness?

CHAPTER ELEVEN
THE VALUE OF RELATIONSHIPS

"Anything is possible when you have the right people there to support you."

— MISTY COPELAND

YOU DON'T HAVE TO DO THIS ALONE. IN THE JOURNEY OF YOUR MENTAL health with the journey of wellness, it's really important that you surround yourself with as much positivity as you can. If you do not feel like you have the right support system in your life, which research has shown that support is a protective factor and have a lot of mental health conditions, then I encourage you to do your best to find different support in your local area or online. There are different organizations who provide support groups to help, which I'll share at the end of the book in the Resources section. Depending on your needs, there are formal mental health support groups, informal Meetup groups, and all sorts of resources, so you don't have to do this journey alone.

It can be really helpful to receive help from someone else, especially when we're talking about this "loneliness pandemic" that is happening right now. It's so important to collaborate. It's so important to be connected. Even if you're in a space where you may not feel like being overly social, you may not feel like going to support groups, or you may not feel like being around a lot of people. If that's the case, think about maybe connecting with a smaller group, or maybe even connecting with one to two people that you trust. That person who you trust can literally be anyone from any walk of your life.

It could be a parent; it could be a child; it could be a coworker; it could be a person from a place of worship. It could be anyone in your life who is meaningful to you and who supports you and your journey, someone who is going to be there for you. Someone who is there for you when times aren't that great, and who's going to be there for you in your happier moments as well. Those are the people to keep close. Those are the people to be grateful for. Those are the people who can help you build yourself up to be the best version of who you are on this planet.

Don't underestimate the power of connection.

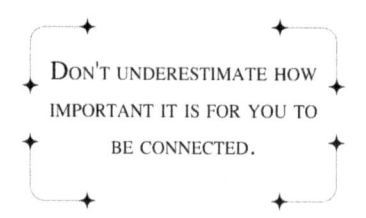

> DON'T UNDERESTIMATE HOW IMPORTANT IT IS FOR YOU TO BE CONNECTED.

Don't underestimate how important it is for you to be connected.

And recognize that this connection can help you in your healing journey and can also help those around you, so stay connected to others, even if there are times when you don't want to socialize with others.

Again, even if you're connected to a smaller group or a few other positive people, that counts in sharing common interests, such as certain arts and crafts, sports, artistic interests, etc. There are more than eight billion people on the planet, so chances are there's something you enjoy doing that someone else enjoys as well. So, connect with like-minded people who can create positive environments for you, which may or may not be those people around you right now. Ask yourself these questions: *Am I in the most supportive environment for me? And if so, where do I need to add more support in my life?*

I encourage you to think about those joyful moments. Think about sharing your joyful moments with someone else. And think about how you and this other person or persons can be uplifting to one another. I remember reading Michelle Obama's book, *The Light We Carry*, and was so excited to read about this notion of the "kitchen table." This was how she brought in her close friends and gained more friends over the years and really had this positive bonding experience with this group of individuals who provided support and helped her carry and shine her light because she absolutely said she did not do this alone. And a lot of you are working so hard in this journey of wellness, working on this journey to be better, and working on this journey to just serve others in all the things that you do, which are all fantastic things. But you also have to be taking care of yourself, and it can be so much easier on your journey to not feel like you're alone and to not do this by yourself.

The Light We Carry was a phenomenal book, and I love that book because it really speaks to how we need to take care of ourselves in order to be the light that we all have inside of us. So, check that book out if you haven't already. And also remember that you do not have to do this journey by yourself. Be well.

Recap

- Don't underestimate the power to connect with someone else in your wellness journey.
- Check out Michelle Obama's book, *The Light We Carry*.
- Ask yourself: Where do I need to add more support in my life right now?

Band-Aid to prevent infection, but you didn't know how to treat that cut on your arm. You could possibly risk leaving this wound open, which does not initially need any hospital intervention, but then the wound becomes infected. Then you have to go to the hospital because of a severe infection. Then you have to stay in the hospital and get treatment for something that could have been prevented. And all you needed to do was to put on some ointment and cover the wound with a Band-Aid. This is exactly how mental health works as well, where prevention can go a long way.

One of the reasons I'm writing this book is because the fact is *mental health education saves lives.* Prevention efforts save lives when you understand and know how to deal with depression or how to deal with anxiety or how to deal with many of the things that are happening in your life. You essentially can have an opportunity to cope with some milder issues and prevent a whole, long, difficult way of receiving treatment or more long-term treatment or something that you didn't even have to go through in the first place.

In my work, I've seen it time and time again. Unfortunately, there are so many kids who were not diagnosed early with a mental health condition, did not have the prevention strategies in place, had so much heartache and pain and suffering unnecessarily because society didn't know how to deal with this child (or families did not have the mental health education they needed to make an informed decision). Because society didn't understand that this child had ADHD, or this child had a learning disability or depression, anxiety or so many other things that were happening.

My advocacy work for mental health, in particular, stems from hearing numerous stories and knowing that there were so many mental health concerns that could have been prevented. So, I want you to understand, the more you educate yourself, the more you can work on decreasing (think control, not cure) different mental health issues. Please do not let this book be the only way that you're educating yourself when it comes to mental health and when it

CHAPTER TWELVE
PREVENTION VS. INTERVENTION

"Embrace the process, trust the process, but most importantly you've gotta respect the process."

— INKY JOHNSON

ONE OF THE DIFFICULTIES WITH THE IDEA OF GETTING BETTER WITH A mental health issue is that we always tend to wait until there's a huge problem, until we're falling apart, until we're so stressed out and overwhelmed instead of thinking instead about prevention efforts. We already know that prevention efforts can help us economically; it can help save money and can help to prevent burnout and even save lives. Prevention tools can help to have a better quality of life, but the problem is we're so focused on waiting until we need an intervention.

Instead, think about how we can prevent issues. Think about if you had a cut on your arm that only needed some ointment and a comes to your wellness. When it comes to your strategies and when it comes to things that you can do in your life to become the best version of who you are. Do not let this book be the only thing, and hopefully it serves as a supplement to other types of research.

I implore you, and strongly encourage you, to understand that you can absolutely devote yourself to prevention strategies in your own life. Remember to make yourself your #1 priority. And as we'll get into in this book, it's also important to understand prevention strategies to help those people around you who may be dealing with a mental health condition. Many of us know someone who's dealing with a mental health issue, so learning ways to help yourself and share this knowledge to help others as well is vital.

The other thing with intervention is sometimes we have wounds that are very deep, right? There are wounds that would require getting stitches, because it's so deep, or an injury might require surgery because it's so severe, and by no means can you put a Band-Aid on it. You cannot put a Band-Aid on a broken arm, right? We know this. You could try, but it's not going to work because you need a stronger intervention, like a cast on your arm.

It's the same thing with mental health. There are certain things that are so severe, so traumatic, and so distressing that it takes a stronger form of treatment and more intensive form of treatment to help. So, some of you may only need to utilize prevention strategies to work with your friends or your family members, and using at-home strategies in this book is enough for you. Some of you need to reach out to a mental health professional, because there are self-help strategies that you've tried for many, many years, and it just hasn't worked or it's just not enough on your own. And that's totally okay.

You can also think of reaching out to a mental health professional as a prevention strategy as well. You don't have to wait until you're falling apart. Sometimes you may reach out to a mental health professional because you need clarity about a life situation. Sometimes you can reach out to a mental health professional because you're dealing with time or stress management difficulties. It doesn't always have to be these chronic conditions. We are falsely believing that therapy is only for people with severe mental health issues, and that's not true! Therapy comes in many different forms, which I'll talk more about in another chapter.

The other good news about prevention efforts is there are so many studies that show there is a better prognosis when you get help earlier, but unfortunately, the National Alliance of Mental Illness (NAMI) showed a study that the average delay between symptom onset and treatment is ELEVEN years (nami.org/mhstats). That's eleven years, on average, of unnecessary suffering, pain, and heartache because of the stigma of mental health, because of the stigma of getting treatment, and because of the thought process of what it means to receive intervention, to receive therapy. It's a heartbreaking statistic! Eleven years!

Thankfully, we're currently in a world that is starting to understand more about mental health treatment and working to reduce the stigma of mental health. And this goes beyond the United States because mental health is a global issue. According to the World Health Organization (WHO), "In 2019, 1 in every 8 people, or 970 million people around the world were living with a mental disorder, with anxiety and depressive disorders the most common…" (who.int/news-room/fact-sheets/detail/mental-disorders) Which is why it's so critically important for us to receive the help we need, which comes in many different forms.

The last thing I'll add about prevention versus intervention is you're giving yourself a gift to work on prevention efforts when you are taking the time to work on who you are as a person. First off, thank you (yes, I'm going to thank you multiple times in this book!). Let me tell you genuinely that I am proud of you. Let me tell you strongly that prevention is about a growth mindset process. Wherever you're at in life, you have to ask yourself: Am I in a place of thriving, or am I in a place of surviving? Maybe you are somewhere in the middle. These are questions that you constantly have to be asking yourself, because one of the best ways to work on thriving is when you understand who you are. This is all a process, and our healing journeys happen in different ways.

I remember when I was in graduate school, it was suggested that the students go to therapy. I'll be honest, I literally went because it was a suggestion for us to go to therapy as a class assignment, for us to experience what therapy was like. So, I went to therapy. Therapy changed my life.

> THERAPY CHANGED MY LIFE.

So, when I went to therapy for what I thought was stress management, I ended up talking about some issues that I was having in my personal life. I didn't even recognize at that time that I had not dealt with my dad not being in my life as a kid, and it was really, really hard for me, but I was so emotionally shut down on that topic, I wasn't even willing to deal with that issue at the time.

But what my therapist did was she planted a seed for me. And that seed ended up meaning that I was able to reconnect with my dad a couple years later (in my early twenties). And I was able to have my dad walk me down the aisle at my wedding (which I always worried, as a little girl, who would walk me down the aisle). I still am able to have a great relationship with my father today because I was able to work on my own healing journey, because it was really difficult not understanding as a child why my dad wasn't in my life at that time. It was a really hard path, and it was also easy to hide my emotions because I was a smart child, doing well in school, and involved in multiple extracurricular activities. (Most people don't check in with youth who "look like everything is fine.") But I can tell you that it was absolutely worth it to make that reconnection with my father, and sometimes our healing comes in many different ways, and in ways that surprise us. Overall, it was a long journey, but it was life- changing.

The other type of inner work that I did was I went to numerous retreats, which was such a healing experience. I attended different healing retreats in different countries, and I absolutely loved the process. I really got to work on my personal development through that method, and retreats can be helpful, depending on your needs and interests.

Connecting with positive family and friends is another way to engage in prevention efforts. There are many studies that show the power of a good support system going a long way in positive mental health. Doing things that are fun, things that bring you joy with those you love, or simply having some heart-to-heart talks can help on your healing experience.

I've read so many self-help books. One of the reasons why I love writing this self-help book for you right now is because I am a "self-help book lover" (which I'm proud to be, by the way!). I absolutely love reading things that are going to better my life. There's no one self-help book that would just cure you; that's not the point. But you can work on reading books to uplift, inspire, motivate, and make you into a stronger person.

Listen to uplifting podcasts. Watch inspirational YouTube videos. Whether you enjoy listening to podcasts, reading books, watching YouTube videos, or whether it is other motivational content that you tune into, make sure you are continuing to build your positive mental state on this healing journey. Those are all the types of things you can do as prevention efforts to build you into a stronger person. There will be many things that you may face in life that are hard. When you work on building yourself up to be the strongest version of yourself, you can mentally prepare to handle life's ups and downs. Let's go!

Recap

- Mental health education saves lives.

- Ask yourself: Am I in a place of thriving or in a place of surviving?
- Prevention strategy examples: reading self-help books, listening to inspirational content, going to therapy, doing inner work through retreats, connecting with family and friends.

CHAPTER THIRTEEN
SELF-LOVE

> "Love yourself first and everything else falls in line. You really have to love yourself to get anything done in this world."
>
> — LUCILLE BALL

ONE OF THE THINGS THAT I'VE SEEN THROUGHOUT MY JOURNEY IN THE mental health field is how much people struggle with this concept of self-love. The reality is, we're all are healing from something. We have to heal from different things at different points in our lives. Some of us are healing from things that have happened in our childhoods. Some of us are healing from things that happened yesterday. And some of us will have to heal from things that are going to happen years from now. Life is always going to give us its ups and downs. Our disappointments, our moments with grief, our moments with shame, and even our moments of happiness … it can all feel like a roller coaster sometimes.

Here are a couple of things for you to think about when it comes to self-love. Number one, if you're stuck in your past, think about what you can do in your journey of self-love to recognize how important it is to love yourself and all that you are, because the reality is your thoughts are only your thoughts. A lot of time when it comes to our journey through self-love, we tell ourselves a lot of things that are not even true. So, it's really critical that you think about working through some of the things that you may have experienced in the past, which has not allowed you to love yourself the way that you need to be loved.

For some of you, that means heading to therapy and receiving counseling. If you're in need of a mental health professional, you can use resources like the American Psychological Association (apa.org) or National Alliance on Mental Illness (nami.org). These organizations have different directories where you can find mental health professionals in your area.

Think about making the investment into the journey of self-love for you. Now, perhaps you are struggling with the future. Meaning you might say, I'm struggling with how not to get caught up with the anxiety of my future. The future is actually an illusion. Meaning we really do not have any idea. Most times, we do not know what the future holds (unless you're a psychic), but anxiety exists about the future, which can really take a toll on your self-love. So how you can love yourself better is you have to understand that you are worthy.

Repeat this aloud often:

I deserve to be happy.
I deserve to be emotionally healthy.
I deserve to have joy.

Because the fact is: You are worthy. You deserve to be happy. You deserve to be emotionally healthy. You deserve to have joy. A lot of times, many of us struggle with worthiness and truly understanding that we're absolutely worthy. It's a journey to love ourselves for who we are. We're allowed to experience happiness. We're allowed to experience joy. And it's not an overnight process to convince yourself of that truth because your mind will play tricks on you, especially when it comes to self-love. You may be dealing with self-hatred, self-doubt, self-blame, guilt, hurt, or confusion because of things that happened decades ago. The reality is you have to allow yourself to be in a state of forgiveness of yourself to be in a state of forgiveness for those around you. And again, there's different levels of mental health in the self-love journey. Everyone's at a different place. So, allow yourself to think about your self-love journey and ask yourself: Can I do this on my own? Do I need a mental health professional? Do I have the resources around me like family and friends to help me get through? Or do I need a combination of these things? The best answer is doing what works for you and proceed with an abundance of self-love.

Recap

- All of us are healing from something.
- Your thoughts are only your thoughts. Just because you think it doesn't always make it true.
- Repeat this aloud often:
- I deserve to be happy.
- I deserve to be emotionally healthy.
- I deserve to have joy.
- Ask yourself: Can I do this on my own? Do I need a mental health professional? Do I have the resources around me like family and friends to help me get through? Or do I need a combination of these things?

CHAPTER FOURTEEN
MENTAL HEALTH DETOX

> "Time never stops. Discomfort is temporary, but the growth on the other side of your discomfort is permanent."
>
> — JEN GOTTLIEB

ONE OF MY MOST FAVORITE THINGS TO DO IS A MENTAL HEALTH DETOX. Often times when you heard the term "detox," you typically think of a physical detox, like how you can rid your body of toxins, right? You may be thinking about how you can refresh or replenish your energy levels and feel healthier and feel better about yourself through this detox. There are a gazillion physical detox products on the market. But also, it's important for you to think about your own mental health detox, which is vital for your healing journey. Because you're always in a different mental place, depending on the season of life that you are in, it's really important to do a mental health detox periodically but intentionally.

So, what is a mental health detox? Well, it's taking a look at your environment and starting to assess what you need to change. Just as how a physical detox would be to rid your body of toxins or different things that's not good for your body. You're also thinking about what you need to get rid of to help your mental health. This can come in the form of changing habits. It can come in the form of assessing the relationships in your life. It can come in the form of things that you're eating, which affect your emotional state. It can come in the form of the amount of exercise you have. And with the mental detox, not only are you taking things out, but you can also add things in.

One of the things I love to do when I have my mental detox is think about my habits and think about ways that I can be the best version of who I am, asking myself the question: *What do I need to change right now to become the best emotionally healthy version of myself?* Your answer to this question might look like taking a social media break. Sometimes that might mean reducing the amount of time you watch television or reducing the amount of time you're spending in activities that do not benefit your mental health. Sometimes that means reducing the amount of time you're spending with individuals in your life who are not good for your mental health. And sometimes it means adding in more positivity, more time for you, more time to work on being the best version of who you are.

Now, it's important to recognize the reason why the mental health detox is important to do on a frequent basis. Your brain starts to accumulate a lot of different experiences, a lot of different thoughts, sometimes negative thoughts, and your brain can accumulate a lot of heavy, stressful emotions, right? You may be trying to process a lot of things and having a difficult time focusing, so you may try to do a "brain dump." As a reminder, a "brain dump" is where you take some time to write down all of the things that come to mind. Whether it's things that you're worrying about, things that you're dealing with, your "to-do" list, things that may lead to you being stressed out and overwhelmed, etc. Write them all down and get them out of your head because temporarily, this can give you a sense of relief to just get your stressors out on paper.

You can do this brain dump in many forms. You can jot down your thoughts in your phone. You can do this on your computer. You can write it down in a journal, to name a few ways. What I tend to do every single day is on my computer, I have these digital notes, and I will just do a brain dump of what I need to do. Maybe categorize it: family things I need to do, work things I need to get done, personal time I need to set aside, etc. After you are done with your brain dump, you can continue to ask yourself questions like: *"What am I doing for my own mental health? How am I doing with self-care? What can I do this day/week/month to increase my level of happiness?"*

Your goal can be for your mental health detox to become a habit, as this is something that you can really think about adding to your toolkit. Just as how you may do a juice cleanse, or some other type of physical detox on a regular basis, you can also add in your mental health detox on a regular basis as well. Just as how you would clear off your desktop on a computer, or you might clear out some old apps on your phone, you also should be aware of clearing out the things, people, situations, or habits in your life that are not best serving your mental health.

Make yourself your #1 priority.

Read that last sentence again.

Say it with me:

I deserve to make myself my #1 priority.
I deserve to be happy.
I deserve to be emotionally healthy.
I deserve to have peace in my life.
I deserve to focus on my mental health.

The other thing about the mental health detox is the timing. Consider making mental health detox a regular routine in your life, but also recognize when you need to be gentle with your heart, mind, body, and your soul. Sometimes you're going through seasons where it's not feasible to do a mental health detox because you feel like you're in survival mode. And that's okay. Get through that time. And remember, this too shall pass.

As you come out of survival mode, and you work on getting back into thriving mode, then you do your mental health detox and work on this as often as you need to for YOU. What your mental health detox looks like will depend on what stage of your life you are in, so your mental health detox that you start today may not look the same five years from now because you will be a different person five years from now. And that's okay. Your goal is mindset growth. And with this mindset growth, your detox will look different.

If someone ate junk food every single day, and they did a physical detox, they might have a lot of stuff clear out. You know what I mean? They might have a lot to clear out of their physical system. However, for a person who eats clean, exercises often, and gets enough sleep, and is doing amazing overall physically and mentally, they can also do a mental health detox, but they just might have less to clear out or maybe they don't have to do the detox as often. So, the frequency of your detox, what your detox consists of for your mental health all depends on what your needs are at that time. Here's wishing you nothing but success on your mental health detox journey. You got this!

Recap

- When starting your mental health detox, ask yourself the question: What do I need to change right now to become the best emotionally healthy version of myself?
- You must prioritize your mental health.
- Choose the frequency of the mental health detox that works for you.
- Say it with me:

MINDSET TRAINING

- I deserve to make myself my #1 priority.
- I deserve to be happy.
- I deserve to be emotionally healthy.
- I deserve to have peace in my life.
- I deserve to focus on my mental health.

PART FIVE
SPIRITUAL SELF-CARE

"It's not important how many times you fall, but your rise after every fall is important. Be the one who stands against every hurdle."

— DR. NEKESHIA HAMMOND

CHAPTER FIFTEEN
SPIRITUAL GROWTH

> "Nothing can dim the light that shines from within."
>
> — MAYA ANGELOU

Growth comes in many forms, and one of the forms is through your spirituality. Now remember, spiritual growth doesn't necessarily have anything to do with religion. It could be connected, but whether or not you feel attached to a particular religion, you still have an opportunity to grow spiritually.

So, what do you need for spiritual growth?

1. You could focus on connecting to the Higher Power, Universe, God, Allah, Jesus ... whatever entity you believe in ... more frequently.
2. Focus on the present moment.
3. Ask for clarity.
4. Stay encouraged and uplifted.

5. Have a mindset that looks for ways to improve your spiritual growth.

Now, I know what you are probably thinking, *I don't have enough time*. But the good news is you can utilize the time that you already have. Just like you, my life gets really busy and hectic too! So, there have been times in car rides alone that I've turned off the music and found myself in prayer and connection with God. I dedicate specific time to a devotional reading each morning. Other times, unplanned throughout the day, just taking a minute to say a prayer for someone in need. And, spiritual growth doesn't necessarily have to mean more prayer; those are just some examples if you believe in the power of prayer.

Taking the time to stay in the present moment and focusing on feeling connected and grounded also can be a part of your spiritual journey. You can feel more grounded by connecting to the Earth, which might come in the form of taking deep breaths, simply sitting in nature, and observing sunsets, sunrises, lakes, beaches, and other natural forms of our Earth. Other people have found "Earthing," the practice of walking barefoot on a surface connected to the Earth (think soil, beaches, natural bodies of water, etc.), to be helpful in their spiritual journeys as well.

Asking for clarity is important too. I've encountered numerous people who are struggling with clarity in life, in response to various life events, and understanding how to make the best decisions and what to do next. Seeking clarity from within is important for your growth journey.

Staying encouraged and uplifted during your spiritual journey may be challenging. When life throws us curveballs, it's normal to feel like giving up on wellness goals. When unexpected changes happen, it can be really hard to stay on track with your spiritual growth journey. These challenging times though are a part of the process, and it is critical during those times to understand how faith can help you get stronger and get you through the emotional pain you may be enduring.

Having a mindset where you are continuing to seek ways to improve your spiritual growth is key. This means finding creative ways to build your spirituality. Remember, you have to do what works for you. When you find the means to utilize the tools and strategy that work in the best way and align with your values, you've won!

When you think about growth mindset, you've probably heard the phrase of growing "emotionally, mentally, physically, and spiritually." We say those terms all the time but are we really taking the time to grow spiritually as well? Ask yourself these questions: *1. What do I need to do today in my spiritual journey to grow closer to a Higher Power? 2. How can I work on grounding techniques to have more spiritual connection? 3. How will my life be different if I grew spiritually?*

Recap

- You choose what your journey looks like: connecting with a Higher Power, focusing on the present moment, seeking clarity, staying uplifted and encouraged, and having a growth mindset for spiritual growth.
- Ask yourself: How would my life be different if I grew spiritually? What can I commit to today to grow closer to a Higher Power?

CHAPTER SIXTEEN
GIVING BACK IS GOOD FOR YOUR MENTAL HEALTH

"Be the change you wish to see in the world."

— GANDHI

GIVING BACK IS ONE OF MY FAVORITE PARTS OF POSITIVE MENTAL HEALTH because it's such an underrated thing to do that can really help your mental health. There are several studies that show the mental health benefits of giving back by showing kindness and compassion, by doing random acts of kindness. There's some really cool websites out there about random acts of kindness and things you can do to help others. There are so many great positive resources about giving back and what it does for your mental health.

I've been absolutely honored to give back to various communities over time, internationally and domestically, with different organizations. And one of the things that's been so amazing to witness and experience was not only my own mental health journey and how giving back has personally and professionally changed me for the better, but also to see others and their journeys and how giving back has helped them to be better with their mental health.

I highly encourage you to ask yourself this question: *How can I help my community?* Studies have shown that when we start to focus on other people by helping others, these positive acts can actually give us a break from worrying about our daily issues or worrying about different things that sometimes we don't even have any control over. (How cool is that?) When we simply take the time to focus on helping others in our communities, we help ourselves as well.

You can think about how you can help a local school. I have a really special place in my heart for helping kids and teens. I think they're the most amazing group of people on the planet because they have so much to learn and so much to offer the world. And when we take the time to teach our youth early, we're giving them a gift into their adult years to understand how they can show up in the world and be the best version of who they are.

I really encourage you to think about how you can help a local school, for example. If you are not sure where to start, you can take a quick moment to call a school and ask what their greatest needs are. Don't make assumptions about what schools need because it really depends on the community. Some schools may need things like school supplies or uniforms for the children, while some schools may need your volunteer hours for a project they are working on.

When you think about giving back, there's a lot of different ways to give back. Sometimes you can give your time. Sometimes you can give your talent, your treasure, your connections, your resources. Get involved with your community interests. Some other questions to ask yourself are: *What am I really passionate about? What is it that will bring me so much joy when I give my time and energy (or perhaps funds) to it as well?*

If you're looking for really great places to donate, I'm going to share with you some of my favorite charities. Feel free to check out their websites. Thank you in advance for anything you can do to help these organizations! My four favorite charities are the following: Ryan Nece Foundation, Rising Media Stars, Inc., Friends of Joshua House, and Big Brothers Big Sisters Tampa Bay.

I will say that I've been on the Board of Directors for the Ryan Nece Foundation for a long time (as of this writing – nine years), and it's been an absolute joy to give my time, energy, and funds to an amazing cause to help the community through different program endeavors. The Ryan Nece Foundation's mission is: "to create opportunities for teens to embrace the Power of Giving through volunteerism and inspirational leadership programs." (https://ryannecefoundation.org/about) I've particularly loved the Student Service Program, which teaches teens and alumni about leadership skills, giving back to the community, personal and professional development skills, and so much more. You can learn more about all the great work the foundation does at ryannecefoundation.org.

I've been on the Board of Directors for Rising Media Stars, Inc. for several years, and I see how much impact they have for women of color in sports broadcasting. "Rising Media Stars' purpose is to provide tools, resources, and opportunities for women of color who are looking to start a career in sports media. It is our mission and goal to diversify the sports broadcasting workforce." (https://www.risingmediastars.org/about). The program has really changed the lives of the program participants and the community. You can check out their website at RisingMediaStars.org.

I've also been a strong supporter of Friends of Joshua House (located in the Tampa Bay area), who help children who have been abused, abandoned, and neglected in the Tampa Bay area. Friends of Joshua House is a group of "...concerned individuals who have dedicated themselves to developing resources to improve the quality of life for abused, abandoned, and neglected children and teens from our community by promoting healing, growth, and empowerment." (https://www.friendsofjoshuahouse.org/about-us/) I had the opportunity to take a tour of their therapeutic residential group homes a few times, and I am so proud of the work they do to help youth. You could check out FriendsofJoshuaHouse.org to learn more about them.

I'm also a supporter of Big Brothers Big Sisters of Tampa Bay, who also has done so much to help our youth through mentorship and helping the community. The mission of BBBS Tampa Bay is "to create and support one-to-one mentoring relationships that ignite the power and promise of youth." (https://bbbstampabay.org/) Their vision to help youth achieve their full potential through mentorship is simply outstanding. You can check them out at bbbstampa.org.

So those are just a few great nonprofits that I've encountered if you are looking for ways to give back.

Now if you're looking for a place in your local community, but you're not sure where to start, here's a couple of tips on how to start giving back. You have to ask yourself what time or amount of money or resources can you dedicate at this time? Now recognize that will change. I'm extremely grateful to have the resources to provide for a lot of different organizations at this time in my life. While I was in graduate school, for instance, I did not have the funds to help organizations in a large monetary way, but I still found the time to volunteer.

Ask yourself: *Where am I, and what can I give?* What about if you are unemployed? You feel like there's no way you can give money right now, because you're in a financial bind. That's fine, but can you donate your time? Or you might say, "I don't have time whatsoever right now, I have so much going on, but I have funds that I can give (wonderful!)"; or you might say, "You know what, I have a lot of connections, and I can help these certain organizations with certain introductions to people or resources." So, we all have something to give that works at that particular time of your life.

Other questions you can ask yourself are: *What is it that I am passionate about, what cause do I truly care about?* In other words, who or what do you want to help? Are you also passionate about children and teens? Are you passionate about mental health? Are you passionate about the environment? Are you passionate about helping people who have food insecurities, or are you passionate about helping people who don't have a place to live or something else?

But just know that the best thing about giving back is you are helping your mental health and physical health, because doing things for others can help you to feel more at peace and with more joy, which can impact different areas of your physical, mental, and emotional health. In whichever way you decide to give back, you can add helping the community to your wellness toolkit. It doesn't matter who you are. All of us have something to give, whether big or small, and every single thing counts. Every single thing counts. Read that last sentence again. Every gesture that you do to help someone counts. So do not be afraid to think that what you have to give is too little because that's not true.

There are many things you can do for those around you, whether it's your family or your friends or strangers. There are random acts of kindness where you can think about engaging in small tasks that have such meaningful impact for others. There are "small" gestures that you may think are no big deal, but to the next person, they could be lifesaving. You never know the true impact of smiling at a stranger as you walk by. You don't know what is going on behind closed doors. You don't know what people are going through. And when people receive a smile, when people think that you care when you're giving back and inserting your positive energy in their lives, it's impactful.

So, it's really important for you to think about giving back. Consider making a list now of random acts of kindness that you can do. I remember one time I was having a really bad day, one of those days where it seemed like everything was going wrong. One of those days where it feels like you spilled something on your shirt, you have a flat tire, and everything is going wrong—one of *those* days. I remember I was going through this drive-thru (I don't even like fast food!), but nonetheless, like I said it was one of those days I had to get my son fed. And I remember that someone in front of me in the drive-thru line bought my meal. When I got to the register to pay, not only did I find out the stranger in front of me bought the meal, but they had given the cashier a note to give to me. And the note said, "Jesus loves you." And I kid you not, I almost burst out into tears because I was having such a bad day, and that was just a small, simple sign to me that everything was going to be okay.

It was a very random act of kindness, a very small gesture. But for me, it was such a needed thing that day. This person had no idea; this was a complete stranger so, of course, they had no idea how my day was going. They had no idea what I was going through. They were just trying to do something kind, but I still remember this from this day, even though this occurred many years ago. I remember how crappy my day was, and how this person took a small amount of time out of their schedule, paid for a fast-food meal, and made this memorable impact for me.

I want you to remember what you think you're doing that is insignificant or "small" is not generally the case. There are studies that show whatever impact you think you're having, it's probably three times as much to the person on the receiving end. So don't stop giving back, and don't stop helping others because these are the type of things not only are we helping our community by doing, but at the end of the day, you're helping your own mental health journey as well.

Recap

- There are mental health benefits of giving back to others.
- Ask yourself: How can I help my community?
- You can give through your time, funds, talent, resources, and connections.

- My favorite charities: Ryan Nece Foundation (ryannecefoundation.org), Rising Media Stars, Inc. (risingmediastars.org), Friends of Joshua House (friendsofjoshuahouse.org), and Big Brothers Big Sisters of Tampa Bay (bbbstampa.org).
- A special thank-you for giving back to the community!

CHAPTER SEVENTEEN
GRATITUDE

"Acknowledging the good that you already have in your life is the foundation for all abundance."

— ECKHART TOLLE

GRATITUDE IS SUCH A COOL, BUT UNDERRATED THING. GRATITUDE IS SO GOOD for your mental health. There's scientific evidence that shows practicing gratitude can positively affect you spiritually, emotionally, mentally, and physically. So why not have a gratitude practice?

There's a lot of ways that you can practice gratitude. One of my favorite ways to practice gratitude started within the last couple of years. I realized I had gotten into a very bad habit of waking up in the morning and heading straight to my cell phone to check Instagram or my email or do some other scrolling that was meaningless in the bigger scheme of life. Sound familiar? It felt like I woke up and as soon as I woke up, there was zero time for myself because I went straight into doing something and trying to respond to an email from the night before or looking at social media and responding to messages. Well, what I realized was that I didn't want to wake up and that'd be the first thing I was doing. So, in my spiritual growth journey, I decided I would instead connect with God first thing in the morning and think about at least one thing that I was grateful for that morning.

Now typically when most people are asked, "What are you grateful for?" they normally say friends, family, health, right? Great things to be grateful for. Those are not bad answers, but it was really important that I didn't wake up every single morning saying the same exact thing, right? So, I decided I wanted to find one unique and specific thing to be grateful for every single morning. I still continue this practice to this day, where as soon as I wake up in the morning, the first thing I do is connect with God, and I go into my gratitude practice, which is to recognize and thank God for one thing that I'm grateful for right now. But please know that the practice of gratitude does not necessarily have to do with your religious beliefs or spiritual beliefs. Gratitude can happen in whatever religion you practice, or don't practice, and in whatever beliefs you have.

Gratitude is available for every single person on the planet. It doesn't matter what your belief system is on that. For me personally, I connect with God as a Christian, but this is open to every single person on the planet no matter what your religious beliefs are. So, in starting this practice, what I found was I had such a renewed sense of gratitude. It was one way to really think about starting my day from the beginning. Even before my day got started, I already started thinking about what I was grateful for. And so, a gratitude practice can be another tool in your toolkit to think about. Continue to ask yourself: *How can I be the best version of myself? How can I work on my own mental health? How can I work on my wellness journey? I know gratitude is important to me, but what am I doing to really be in that mindset of gratitude?*

Another way that you can practice gratitude is with gratitude journals, which there are so many apps for right now. If you enjoy physically writing out your thoughts, you can write down three things you're grateful for every day. There are apps out there where you can write in what you're grateful for you, or you can have a practice of recognizing people who have been good to you and giving them the recognition they deserve. Meaning thanking people often for what they've done for you. I still like old school thank-you cards to give out. At Hammond Psychology & Associates, our families who receive evaluations get a personalized thank-you card as a reminder of how important they are and our gratitude for them choosing our practice. I really enjoy thanking people because when people experience being thanked, it can also help their mental health as well. There's a lot of people who you just don't know what they're going through. So, what you think is a small thank-you is actually a really big deal to them. You can literally take twenty seconds to send someone a quick thank-you text message, which counts too! Or can you thank someone through email ... or even send them an old school thank-you card via snail mail. There's no wrong way to thank someone.

The other piece about gratitude is that gratitude allows you to shift your mindset and really think about the blessings that you have in your life. Because the reality is, we are so consumed oftentimes with the negativity around us. There are moments when you may feel like the world is falling apart. It can feel like you're so overwhelmed, and you may be at a dark point in your life. But when you work on your gratitude, then you start to recognize that there are a lot of things that may be going well and a lot of things that you can be grateful for.

And if you're in a dark time right now where you're like, "I can't think of anything to be grateful for," be grateful that you're alive.

> AND IF YOU'RE IN A DARK TIME RIGHT NOW WHERE YOU'RE LIKE, "I CAN'T THINK OF ANYTHING TO BE GRATEFUL FOR," BE GRATEFUL THAT YOU'RE ALIVE.

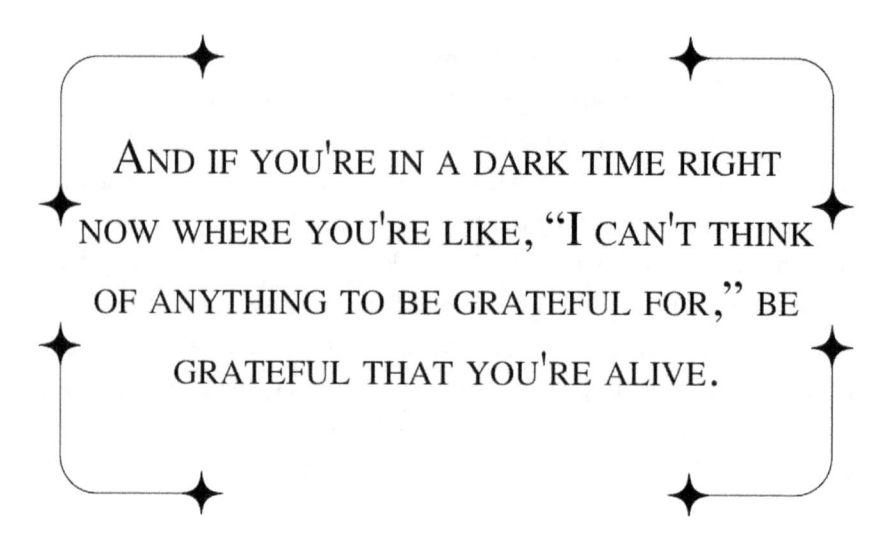

If you're reading this book right now, or you're listening to this book right now, then you are very blessed to have that experience to be listening or to be reading something that allows you to work on being a better version of who you are.

So, it's really important to have those spaces of gratitude. Gratitude for who you are. Gratitude for where you're going. Gratitude for your experiences that have shaped you into the person that you are today. Gratitude for getting through your darkest hours. Gratitude for being alive. And, at the end of the day, you have to be grateful for life itself.

As I wrap up the gratitude chapter, I want to express my gratitude to you for taking the time to read this book, for taking the time to learn how to be better emotionally, spiritually, mentally, physically, and for taking the time to allow yourself to contemplate all of the ways that you can work on your mental health. **You are so much stronger than you know.** And you're so much wiser than you know, and blessed. And you have a lot of opportunity to continue in your growth.

I'd like to thank you from the bottom of my heart for getting this far in the book and taking the time to work on yourself. I'm proud of you. The mental health and wellness journey is not always the easiest for each and every one of us. But there are a lot of opportunities and resources that we can utilize to work on our own healing journeys and work on our own transformations. So, thank you for being you. If no one has told you today, I'm super proud of you for you taking the time to heal and for you allowing yourself to know that you deserve self-care.

You deserve to have a healthy mind. You deserve to be a better version of who you are. You deserve to live a happy and fulfilled life. Thank you for reading, and I wish you so much happiness and success in all that you do.

Recap

- Start a daily gratitude practice.
- Gratitude allows you to shift your mindset and focus on the positive aspects of your life.
- Ask yourself: What am I doing to stay in a mindset of gratitude?

CHAPTER EIGHTEEN
HELPING OTHERS

"But when we look for the good in others, we start to see the best in ourselves too."

— JAY SHETTY

YES, I KNOW THIS BOOK IS ALL ABOUT HELPING YOU TO BE THE BEST VERSION of who you are and helping with your own mental health conditions or challenges, or just working on your own well-being. But it's also important to think about how you can support someone else in your life who may have mental health challenges. Believe it or not, there are so many studies that show how helping other people can benefit your own mental health, and also, it may alleviate some stress that you're having. When you think about people in your life who are having mental health difficulties, ask yourself how you can support them because there are a lot of different ways you can support someone else with a mental health issue.

Number one: Don't make assumptions. The problem is that

when you make an assumption about someone with a mental health issue, just because of their diagnosis, you are doing them a disservice. If you hear the term depression, anxiety, ADHD, bipolar disorder, schizophrenia, etc., what is the first thing that comes to mind for you? Take thirty seconds to think about what is the first thing that comes to mind.

If someone told you that they had any of those diagnoses, you probably would have an image or a thought or a belief about those conditions. Some of your beliefs about mental health are absolutely not true! These are <u>myths</u>. These are inaccurate statements. I can tell you that of the thousands of people I've spoken with who have various mental health conditions, many people may have the same exact label, but many people with the same exact condition have totally different lives. Totally different expressions of depression, anxiety, bipolar disorder, ADHD, or any other condition that they're going through. Because the fact of the matter is we all have a different story.

We all have a different journey. So that being the case, if we all have a different journey and we all have a different experience, then we should not make assumptions about when people tell us they have depression or anxiety or bipolar disorder, or whatever the condition is they have. So critically important, so please do not make assumptions.

Number two: Do not blame yourself. Self-blame is common, especially if you're close to that person who has a mental health condition or issue. But I want you to remember that the best thing you could do for this person is for you to work on yourself, not to blame yourself. Maybe you're a parent, maybe you're an aunt or uncle, a sister, or a brother, or in some way connected to this person that has a mental health condition. And you may think that it's your fault, but it's probably not. So, work within yourself to not have self-blame and shame, but instead work to get to a healed place so you can be in a place of support for them. Because support comes in many different forms. The first step is not making assumptions. The second thing is to think about not blaming yourself.

Number three: Engage in deep listening. When you really listen to a person and you hear their story, and when you do your best to understand, even though you may never have walked a day in the life of this person, you can better understand their perspective. You may learn that this person experienced trauma, which led to some negative behavior due to the trauma. You don't have to exactly experience the same life as them to have empathy, compassion, and kindness toward them. You don't have to have the same exact life. But when you extend a listening ear, it could mean the world to this person.

Now, there are some people that want so badly to tell you about their pain and their heartache or what they're going through. And there are other people who absolutely have no desire to share their life stories with you. So, respect the level of what people want to share with you about their lives, but if they do want to share their mental health journeys, be in a supportive state to hear what they have to say.

Number four: Respect where people are at in their journeys and do your best to support them. If the person is open to it, you can offer them mental health resources. You can offer them your personal support, along with offering them places for therapy, or you can offer them ideas of how they can deal with their own wellness journeys or deal with their own difficulties. If that person is not open to receiving any type of treatment, then you do the best that you can to listen and support them at their current mental and emotional state. You do the best that you can to check in because the reality is the checking-in that we do with people has a stronger effect than we know of. You may think you're simply sending a text message or an email or phone call, or in whatever manner you're checking with someone just to say, "Hey, are you okay? Hey, how are you doing? Hey, do you need anything?"

You may think that checking in on them is so small. But I can tell you there are so many people I've met who checked in with someone and ended up saving their life. It has saved their lives because they've said, "Man, someone actually cares about me."

And here's the thing. You may even think that person doesn't care because that person may never ever express to you a thank-you. That's okay. Don't look for a thank-you. Instead, just do what you need to do to check in with that person and plant a seed for them. Do what you need to do to be supportive of that person. Sometimes it's hard because you want so badly to help someone who's not in the mindset to receive the help they need, which can be really hard, really challenging. But in that time, you need to do your best to take care of you. The fact is there are some people just at certain seasons of their lives that don't want help and then later decide they are ready to receive help. And sadly though, there are some people who will never ever accept help that they need on a professional level. But that doesn't mean they can't still receive the support around them, whether the support is from family, friends, or the community.

The other thing to keep in mind is that it's important for us as a community to be thinking about impacting other people's lives, whether you're a teacher, whether you're a parent, whether you're a community member or whatever role you plan. The reason why it's so important for us to be connected, reaching out, and providing support to show you care about this person is because there are so many people, so many kids, so many families who will NEVER receive the mental services that they need. We already have plenty of data, plenty of research statistics to show that so many people will never receive the help they deserve and need because of the stigma of mental health. Because of the lack of funds, because of difficulties with insurance companies, because of a distrust of the mental health system, and the list goes on and on. People may never ever receive those professional mental health services but if you are a resource, if that is all they have, then be that life-changing force for them. *One person can make a difference in someone's life.*

There are so many teacher groups that I've spoken with, and I'm so grateful to speak with them because of how vital teachers are for our youth. Teachers have this incredible opportunity. If you are a teacher reading this, then just remember that you are around these children or teens every single day, oftentimes spending more time with them than their own family members. So, you have an opportunity to pour into them. You have an opportunity to make sure that you check in with them, and you have an opportunity to allow them to experience kindness and compassion in their lives.

Because the reality is you don't know how someone may be suffering, and you may not know the mental health challenges that they face. You don't know how people are not showing up for them. You don't know their trauma. You don't know their life story. You don't know any of those things. But you have an opportunity to treat people with kindness, to be compassionate, and to help them heal on their journey. Trust me, there are so many times when you don't know how your positive actions are helping someone. That is the reality.

We are literally at the place of our lives right now where your patience, your grace, and your kindness are helping people in life and helping to heal people. We don't talk about this enough. This is a really important chapter, and I'm glad that you're reading this chapter and you've gotten this far. Because we respectfully don't recognize how important this is when we're talking about mental health, like how important this is to think about the impact each of us have on the well-being of others.

We always think about the big type of interventions, which are important and needed, but hear me when I say this. What about the millions and millions of people who will never have any mental health treatment? You know who they are. They will never receive treatment because they don't believe in therapy. They're not going to go to therapy because therapy is too expensive, or whatever excuse they use as a reason. What about those people? What about those kids? What about those families who still deserve to have a higher quality of life too? They still deserve to be happy; they still deserve to be emotionally healthy, right?

If you could support these people that you may know who you may even suspect that they're dealing with someone or they're struggling with their mental wellness in some way. They may be dealing with something where they have so much trauma, so much hurt, so much pain, you might not know for sure. But if you even suspect that that is happening, please reach out to them.

We have a gift that we can give to someone by simply supporting them. And I want you to ask yourself these questions. *What space am I in right now? Am I in a space where I can be a light to someone else? Or am I in a space where I'm working on my own healing journey and I'm so depleted and so overwhelmed?* And here's the reality. Our mental health capacity shows up on a continuum. You could be in both of those spaces, and that's okay.

If you gave yourself a percentage, you might have more of yourself to give at any season of your life where you can really be a light to someone else, and when you can really free someone and really uplift someone. And you may be in a place where you are like, "Man, I'm really in a dark place right now. And instead, I need to work on me so much," which is okay. "But then when I do get to that stronger place mentally, physically, emotionally, and spiritually, when I get to that stronger place, then I'm going to do what I need to do to help other people." So really think about for you, what space are you in? Decide what level and effort you can devote to helping others in this season of your life.

I'm writing this book, and my life is far from perfect, but I'm in a better place emotionally, spiritually, mentally, and physically because I worked for *years* on personal development. With the help of people around me, I've had amazing people in my life. Because of these incredible people in my life, I had an opportunity to dive deep and work on my own healing journey (and I still do!). I love sharing these wellness practices with you, professionally and personally. I'm sharing these practices with you so you can think about how you can help yourself but also how you can help other people when you're ready to be in that space. It's all about asking yourself often what you can give.

You have to give to yourself, and you can give to others as well. Self-care is not selfish. Please put yourself first, but also you can be in a space to provide light to others, because you can be in a space to help free others. You can be in a space to help people feel better. *You don't have to be a mental health professional to be supportive of the people in your lives.*

When I first started graduate school, I remember there was almost this notion I made up that I thought I knew the solution to helping people. *Everybody just needs therapy,* I wrongly thought. *Mental health professionals need to just get to as many people as possible.* But then I realized throughout my career that mental health professionals are only a small part of the solution. We are literally only a small part of the solution. The reality is it takes a community. They say it takes a village to raise a child. Well, it takes a ginormous village then to raise the whole population. It takes a village to help everyone who feels stressed out or overwhelmed or burdened from the day-to-day demands.

The COVID-19 pandemic started not too long ago and brought with it unique challenges that many are still suffering from. Many of us went through so many unexpected changes. A lot of us are still healing. You're reading this book years and years later, and there are still many of you who are healing emotionally from the pandemic. There are still many people who are dealing with loneliness.

The U.S. Surgeon General produced an advisory due to the loneliness pandemic. According to HHS.gov's article "New Surgeon General Advisory Raises Alarm about the Devastating Impact of the Epidemic of Loneliness and Isolation in the United States" (5/3/23):

This Surgeon General's advisory lays out a framework for the United States to establish a National Strategy to Advance Social Connection based on six foundational pillars:

1. **Strengthen Social Infrastructure:** Connections are not just influenced by individual interactions, but by the physical elements of a community (parks, libraries, playgrounds) and the programs and policies in place. To strengthen social infrastructure, communities must design environments that promote connection, establish and scale community connection programs, and invest in institutions that bring people together.
2. **Enact Pro-Connection Public Policies:** National, state, local, and tribal governments play a role in establishing policies, like accessible public transportation or paid family leave, that can support and enable more connection among a community or a family.
3. **Mobilize the Health Sector:** Because loneliness and isolation are risk factors for several major health conditions (including heart disease, dementia, depression), as well as for premature death, health care providers are well-positioned to assess patients for risk of loneliness and intervene.
4. **Reform Digital Environments:** We must critically evaluate our relationship with technology and ensure that how we interact digitally does not detract from meaningful and healing connection with others.
5. **Deepen Our Knowledge:** A more robust research agenda, beyond the evidence outlined in the advisory, must be established to further our understanding of the causes and consequences of social disconnection, populations at risk, and the effectiveness of efforts to boost connection.
6. **Cultivate a Culture of Connection:** The informal practices of everyday life (the norms and culture of how we engage one another) significantly influence the relationships we have in our lives. We cannot be

successful in the other pillars without a culture of connection.

Excerpt from https://www.hhs.gov/about/news/2023/05/03/new-surgeon-general-advisory-raises-alarm-about-devastating-impact-epidemic-loneliness-isolation-united-states.html

Feeling loneliness, feeling distress, feeling the depression or anxiety, and all these types of things is tough. So, for you to be reaching out to someone, for you to be impacting someone positively by simply reaching out to them, that's very powerful. And let me remind you that small gestures sometimes have tremendous impact and way more impact than you know. For you to simply help someone, you're essentially working on saving people's lives. And as big of a role as that seems to be is literally the reality that we're in right now.

I want to say strongly that I commend you for reading this chapter. I absolutely am so excited for you to take what you're learning and to help other people. This is what this chapter is all about. It cannot just fall on mental health professionals to save the state of the world. Yes, we want to put on our capes, right? We want to save so many people and to help so many people. That's why a lot of mental health professionals go into the field to help others, but the reality is every single one of us on this planet has an opportunity to help someone out. So, thank you for what you're doing. Thank you for showing up for those around you. Thank you for being a support system. Thank you for being who you are. Continue to think about how you can help people around you, which can be therapeutic for their mental health and yours. Trust the process.

Recap

- Four tips to help others: 1. Don't make assumptions, 2. Do not blame yourself, 3. Engage in deep listening, 4. Respect people where they are in their journeys.
- One person can make a difference in someone's life.
- You have an opportunity to help people on their healing journeys through kindness and compassion.

PART SIX
CONCLUSION

"It's never too late to learn something new! Keep learning, keep growing."

— DR. NEKESHIA HAMMOND

CHAPTER NINETEEN
LIFETIME COMMITMENT

"People often say that motivation doesn't last. Well, neither does bathing – that's why we recommend it daily."

— ZIG ZIGLAR

OUR JOURNEY INTO WELLNESS AND WELL-BEING IS SOMETIMES COMPARED TO living the motto, "Life is a marathon." A marathon is 26.2 miles. A marathon, for most people, takes hours, and then you're done with the race. Maybe you're walking or running it, with a certain goal of time or just to complete it. So, it takes a varying amount of time depending on the person's ability levels, but generally it doesn't take more than a day to complete a marathon. Well, when it comes to making a commitment to your mental health and your well-being, life is *not* a marathon. None of the strategies in this book can be done in a day. They say Rome wasn't built in a day; well neither is your mindset growth, because the reality is that it absolutely takes a lifetime commitment to build up who you are. This is an ongoing process.

On a recent *Mental Health Moment with Dr. Hammond* episode, I talked about burnout prevention. We had an interesting discussion from people across the globe about burnout prevention efforts. And we delved into this idea that the life changes you want to make are all part of an ongoing process, which might sound overwhelming. But here's the good news.

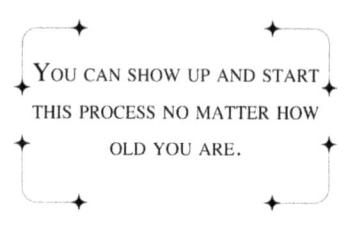

> You can show up and start this process no matter how old you are.

I taught my son about his mental health and wellness strategies, deep breathing, all those fun things when he was in preschool. (I'm sure he loves having a mom as a psychologist ... I'll ask him when he's older.) But the point is it's never too early to start these conversations. And I don't care if you're reading this right now and you're ninety-two years old. It's never too old to start. This is all a process.

Unlike a marathon, where you have a certain day, you have to show up at a certain time, and you have to be done with the race by a certain time, it doesn't work like that when it comes to your well-being. You get to start whenever the time is right for you. You could be telling yourself, *Man, you know, I've had a really difficult life. This has been hard. I haven't done what I need to do for myself.* That's completely okay; you can still make the adjustments needed for your wellness. In the words of the late great Maya Angelou, she said, "Do the best you can until you know better, then when you know better, do better." Now that you know you can empower yourself to take the steps to start implementing the things that you need for your life, remember: Life is not (always) a marathon. But we can decide when to run our races. And some of the time you're going to run a race and you're going to run into obstacles.

I remember when I used to run half marathons, and I recall vividly that there was so much mental preparation that had to be done for the task. It even felt like sometimes you had to be more mentally prepared than physically because you had to prepare for different parts of the race. You had to think about your hydration; you had to think about what pace you were going to run; you had to think about the type of clothing and shoes to endure the 13.1 miles, and many other things to prepare. You also had to think about the internal dialogue that you would have with yourself for the race. I recalled so many times during races that I would want to stop running mid-race. So, when I would run the half marathons, what would happen to me is I would get to a point where I would "hit the wall" (mentally just being drained), and I would start to tell myself that I was tired or ask myself why in the world was I running 13.1 miles anyway, or remember when I would drive on the highway and how long 13.1 miles felt.

Well, I remember this one race that I'll never forget, where I wanted to earn a PR (personal record). I ran and got to like mile two (yes, only 2 miles of the 13.1 miles) and really wanted to give up. I just didn't feel like I had it in me that day. Well, another fellow runner came by, and he said, "Hey, what's your pace?" And I say "Well, I really want to run this in under two hours," and he said, "Okay, come on. Yeah, I can help you with that. Let me run with you for a little bit." And I was really happy for the generosity of a stranger. It was a small thing in the larger scheme of life, but it was a big deal to me at the time to earn the PR. And so I ran with him a couple miles, and he helped to pace me. And sure enough, that was one of my best races ever. I did hit my goal of running the half marathon in well under two hours. And it was just so crazy to me because one of the things that was important as a part of that story is that I had someone, a random stranger, who just wanted to help out. He didn't even know what I was going through mentally, but he brought kindness and compassion, and he helped me get to that goal because I was about to give up. I really felt like I was seriously about to give up and just walk for the rest of the race.

So, be reminded that on this journey of well-being, not only is this a lifelong commitment but thankfully, you will have people along the way in your journey who show up for you. There's going to be times when people will show up who are complete strangers, and there will be times when your friends and family may choose to show up for you also. You may have already had this happen to you in different areas of your life.

When I think back to the preparation with the races, there always seemed like there was something to prepare for, like thinking about hydration, for instance. Do you have enough water? Are you drinking enough water? Are you hydrating ahead of time? Do you have everything you need? Are you prepared? In real life, there's a lot of things we have to prepare for, but there's other life events that pop up unexpectedly.

If you've ever had a loss where you knew ahead of time that you were losing someone in your life, sometimes you can try to mentally prepare. It can still be overwhelming, but you have a chance to prepare. Sometimes you know ahead of time that you're going to have a loss in a relationship or you're going to have a loss of a job or some other type of stressful transition.

Other times, life changes happen that you never expected: sometimes shocking, sometimes sad, sometimes joyful, and so on. We can prepare ourselves if we know the day and time of the race. The fact is there's mental and physical training for racing to prepare the body and mind to handle a task.

Depending on the training, the outcome can be affected. It's similar to your mental health and wellness. Think about how you're preparing yourself for this lifetime journey of positive well-being. Knowing that there are people who will show up for you, there are people who are going to be complete strangers. There are people who are going to be your family, your friends, your coworkers, someone from your place of worship, or whomever else, but there are a few who are just there for you in your life at different seasons. And hopefully you express your gratitude as often as you can to the strangers or friends, family, coworkers, or whomever else supports you in this process.

If you feel alone right now, and you don't feel like there is anyone to support you, please know that there is a network of mental health professionals across the globe, there are hotlines to call to talk to someone, and there are many reputable online support groups and forums. (You can find these resources in the mental health resources at the end of this book.) You also have the opportunity to really get to know and love yourself. Maybe you believe in a Higher Power, or maybe you have to rely a little bit on yourself in this season of your life. Either way, there's always a way for you not to feel alone in this journey. It is important for you to stay connected to something and/or someone.

In conclusion, the journey into wellness and positive well-being is not a marathon. This healing journey is not a one-day event. You get to set the pace that works for you because your healing progress is so important. Once you show up for yourself fully, you can utilize your coping mechanisms to work through life's ups and downs. You can even use a mantra to get through the difficult internal dialogue. My mantra when I used to run long races was to constantly tell myself, "Keep going. Keep going. Keep going." Because there were so many times in that race, no matter how physically prepared I was, where hitting the wall mentally seemed to happen. But then, I managed to push through, and the race did eventually end.

I remember I would ask myself: *Why in the world am I running these races anyway?* I would tell myself, "I'm tired. I don't feel like doing this. I don't feel like doing this today. Why am I here, what's the point?" Like all these negative things, but I had time to repeat my mantra, "Keep going, keep going, keep going," which later led me to my philosophy in life: "Keep going. Keep growing." A lot of things that we go through, we have to understand that these are for our growth. What's happening is happening not "to us," but "for us," to help us in our journey of growth. Make the lifetime commitment to your growth. Cheers!

Recap

- The journey into well-being is NOT a one-day marathon.
- Allow people to support you along the path.
- What is your word or phrase in life to get you through the tough times?

CHAPTER TWENTY
THERAPY OPTIONS

> "Optimism is the faith that leads to achievement. Nothing can be done without hope and confidence."
>
> — HELEN KELLER

There are many different types of therapy, which I am going to describe various types of therapy in this chapter. However, these therapies are by no means an all-inclusive list. If you think you will need therapy, please reach out to a mental health professional to help you understand the best option for your situation. One of the common questions I get asked as a psychologist is "Does everyone need therapy?" Well, the reality is – they don't.

Every person on the planet does not *need* to go to psychotherapy. There are eight billion people on the planet, and the reality is there's not enough mental health professionals to fulfill that need. But, yes, all eight billion people deserve to have happiness, be emotionally healthy, and fulfilled (by their own definition of being happy and fulfilled).

Therapy comes in different forms, with an initial thought process that tends to happen. And it looks like really assessing or understanding who is the therapy for. There are things that happen in our lives that could require individual therapy, meaning therapy that's only between you and a therapist (one on one).

You may be talking about a lot of different issues, whereas most of the time people think of therapy as what they've seen on television, the stereotypical patient who lays on the couch and talks about all their childhood problems. While some types of therapy are discussing issues about your childhood and resolving different issues, there are also many different types of therapies where the focus is not on your childhood issues. Therapy comes in different forms.

The type of therapy that fits best depends on the issues you are working on, whether it's cognitive behavioral therapy, dialectical behavioral therapy, solution-oriented therapy, etc. There are so many different therapies now that incorporate art. There's hip-hop therapy and various therapies that incorporate dance. There are a lot of different types of therapy, but the most important thing is to do what works for you. Maybe you say, "I don't know what works for me," which is why then you can have a discussion with a mental health professional who will look at some of the things that you're dealing with and know what best supports your needs for therapy. This is so that you can get the help you need to get better.

Then there's group therapy. Is group therapy for everyone? Absolutely not. With group therapy, there are a lot of different types of groups for a lot of different types of reasons. There's supportive group therapy; there's anger management; there's social skills therapy; there's therapy for group therapy for all sorts of different mental health conditions, physical health conditions, etc.

In today's digital age, there's online group and tele-health therapy. The most important thing to recognize is that the group therapy is really up to you and what you need to feel better. For some people, they need to process emotions or process trauma or feel more supported by other people who understand their journeys. That can be really helpful. There's therapy for new moms, there's postpartum depression therapy, or maybe it's therapy for chronic mental or physical health illness, like lupus or cancer support treatments, and the list goes on and on.

The most important question to ask yourself is: *Am I the type of person who needs other people that have been through similar circumstances to help me process or is this something, a journey, I want to take on my own?* It's a matter of finding the best fit for you.

How do you know if the therapist that you choose is the best therapist for you? There are many different things to consider.

One of the things to consider is if you can connect with the other person.

Because the reality is a person can have the biggest accolades or go to the best universities out there or have the best resume. But if you don't connect with this person, if you don't feel a sense of connection

> ONE OF THE THINGS TO CONSIDER IS IF YOU CAN CONNECT WITH THE OTHER PERSON.

and trust, it's going to be really hard to get the healing that you need. So, asking yourself if you are really connecting with this person and does this person have the experience that you need is really important.

For individuals from diverse backgrounds, one of the biggest concepts that we talk about now in the mental health field is this idea of cultural competence. So, it is also critical that you are finding someone who is culturally competent, whichever culture you come from or whichever belief system you live by. There are all sorts of different types of therapy, whether it's Christian-based therapy or based on a certain religion or based on certain expertise in your area. The biggest reminder is to make sure that you feel understood by your mental health provider.

The therapy process can also include a combination of not just therapy, but there are individuals who decide to have traditional psychotherapy along with medication, or along with different types of practices, such as biofeedback and other methods. These other methods can be done in conjunction with therapy to really round out the treatment experience, depending on what level of depression or anxiety or whatever mental health condition that you're experiencing.

When it comes to wellness, or when it comes to mental health or well-being, there are issues that you will experience that are mild, moderate, or severe. The conditions may all have different levels of need, and the intervention depends on the level of severity of the symptoms.

The other thing about different treatment approaches is a lot of times I asked - does diet matter? It absolutely does matter. Most people agree that it is vital to eat healthy and take care of your body, along with getting enough sleep. In addition to nutrition, whether you want to add in yoga practices, meditation, or all sorts of other wellness things, like sound baths, sound therapy, there's so many things out there that you could try. I like trying different things related to wellness often. Because again, I have to do my best like everyone else on the planet to stay uplifted, to stay motivated. I frequently think about my wellness because especially with my crazy, busy, hectic schedule like everyone else, it's so important. I cannot do what I do without taking care of myself (and I still vividly remember life before making a commitment to self-care. Long story short, it wasn't pretty).

So yes, exercise is important, diet is important, as well as various types of mental health interventions, like individual therapy or family therapy. There may be a family member or two or a whole group of family where you all need to go into therapy sessions and process a situation and learn how to communicate better.

There are various therapy options out there to best meet your situational needs. Of course, there's also marital therapy or couples therapy, if you're dealing with a relationship issue that you need to work on being a stronger entity together, or work on communication skills or work on conflict skills or whatever it is that has occurred that you need to process through, heal through, or just have a better quality of life in that area.

Another type of therapy is parent skills therapy. For example, parent sessions where you can work on ways for you to learn how to deal or cope with maybe a child or family member who is having some mental health issues and you want to know how best to support them.

I remember hearing Jen Gottlieb speak several times at conferences and remind the crowd to "Start before you're ready." Jen is a "...powerhouse entrepreneur, international speaker, [podcast host], and co-founder of Super Connector Media..." (jengottlieb.com/about) Reach out to a mental health professional if you don't have everything figured out in your healing journey. Take a shot on yourself. The good news is that there are a lot of different times of therapy, and you can find the therapy that best supports your needs. Therapy is absolutely not a "one size fits all" approach.

Recap

- There are many different types of therapy, depending on your needs: individual, group, family, couples, marital, and more.
- Choose the therapist that you feel is most qualified to attend to your wellness goals and you connect with the best.
- You can always supplement therapy with other forms of mental health treatment (medication, change of diet, change of lifestyle, alternative wellness programs).

CHAPTER TWENTY-ONE
THE SEED

"Life is an opportunity, benefit from it. Life is beauty, admire it. Life is a dream, realise it."

— MOTHER TERESA

I WANT TO CONGRATULATE YOU FOR GETTING THIS FAR IN THE BOOK. MOST people who start books don't finish them—but YOU did! See? You have it in you to do what most can't.

However, reading a book and applying the new knowledge are two separate issues. Knowing how to bake a cake only gets people cake if they exercise their knowledge and bake it.

I'd like for you to take a moment and envision how your life would be in 12 months having applied the teachings of this book. Go ahead. Close your eyes and visualize the life you would live if you cared for yourself the way you should, if you stopped talking bad about yourself and fed yourself positive self-talk, if you cleared your mental clutter, if you found inner peace, if you gave yourself permission to heal from yourself and those who have done things to you, if you put more value into your most important relationships, if you grew spiritually, and if you gave back in your own way.

How much happier would you be?
How much better would your relationships be?
How would people think of you?
What could it do to your career?
How much better would you sleep?
How much better would you feel physically?
How much more confident would you be?
How much more would people enjoy your company?
How much calmer would you be?
How much more focused would you be?
How much more impactful would you be?
How much more fulfilled would you be?

Anxiety, stress, burnout, and confusion are emotions we all deal with, but imagine a life where you control all of that. Imagine a life with enough time to work on you and your dreams. Imagine the looks of approval and love from those important to you.

I want to share a secret I hope you know: You can live that life.

I'll go even deeper; you are supposed to live that life. Somewhere, somehow, you lost your true self and maybe even stopped dreaming of being happier, sexier, and more successful.

It's time to get it back, my friend.

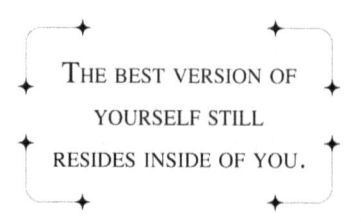

> The best version of yourself still resides inside of you.

The best version of yourself still resides inside of you.

It's been yelling to come out but the sounds of the world and responsibilities have out-shouted it. No more. You deserve to give yourself the best life you can and, in the process, show up powerfully for those you love. I know you can.

If you'd like to explore this content further, please visit my site and take the Self Care Masterclass I prepared for you: www.mindsettrainingclass.com. Allow me to give you a little hand-holding through this course and help you get started on the right path to taking control of your life.

The foundation has been laid. A seed has been deposited in your mind and spirit. Water and nurture the seed and grow into the fantastic, happy, productive human being you were created to be!

ABOUT THE AUTHOR

Dr. Nekeshia Hammond is a distinguished psychologist, executive coach, and the visionary founder of Hammond Psychology & Associates, a private practice in the Tampa Bay area. Widely recognized for her profound insights into mental health, burnout prevention, and leadership development, Dr. Hammond is also the esteemed host of the acclaimed series "Mental Health Moment with Dr. Hammond."

Having served as the former President of the Florida Psychological Association, Dr. Hammond's impact extends beyond clinical practice to pivotal roles on the boards of the Ryan Nece Foundation and Rising Media Stars, Inc. Her remarkable dedication to mental health advocacy and community empowerment has garnered her numerous prestigious awards, including the Next Level Leadership Award, the Brian Thomas Spirit of Excellence, and the President's Lifetime Achievement Award.

Dr. Hammond's expertise has been sought after by international audiences, as she captivates listeners as a distinguished speaker and Amazon international best-selling author. Her profound influence transcends traditional boundaries, with features on major media platforms such as NBC, ABC, CBS, FOX, and Essence Magazine.

Renowned for her dynamic presentations, Dr. Hammond has graced illustrious stages including Corporate Counsel Women of Color and TEDx, where she shares her holistic approach to mental wellness and leadership equilibrium. She is also the author of "The Practical Guide to Raising Emotionally Healthy Children" and "ADHD Explained: What Every Parent Needs to Know."

Beyond her professional endeavors, Dr. Hammond finds joy in cherished moments with her husband and son. She finds fulfillment in a diverse array of interests, including nature walks, leisure writing, international exploration, and CrossFit.

For speaking engagements or media consultations, Dr. Hammond can be reached through her website: www.DrNekeshiaHammond.com.

You can also follow her on social media:

IG: @Dr.Hammond
FB and LinkedIn: Dr. Nekeshia Hammond
Twitter: @Dr_Hammond

ACKNOWLEDGMENTS

First and foremost, thank you God for giving me the strength and wisdom to serve as a vessel and be able to provide hope and inspiration for so many people in my life. I am honored and humbled to serve to help others on their life journeys.

To my husband, Laurence, thank you for being my rock. Thank you for your patience as I always seem to juggle a million things, but you have been instrumental in my wellness journey and an incredible dad to our son.

To my son, Laurence Jr., I appreciate you being outstanding! You never cease to amaze me with your beautiful and kind personality. I feel like the luckiest person in the world to have you as my son.

To my family–thank you for being with me on this journey of life and your support through my childhood and adult years is very meaningful.

To all of my friends, especially Lalita and Christina, I so appreciate your love and support always. I'm blessed to have you all in my life.

To every colleague I've encountered–just know that you've inspired me much more than you realize.

To all of my team members with Hammond Psychology & Associates, you all are such a joy to work with and truly embody the saying that "Teamwork makes the dream work." THANK YOU!

To the Florida Psychological Association, Ryan Nece Foundation, and Rising Media Stars, Inc.–it has been an honor to serve on your board of directors—the experience of giving my time and energy to your missions has been a blessing and nourishing to my soul.

To Ryan Nece, thank you for teaching me about the Power of Giving in all that you do to help the community. You inspire me greatly with how you show up as a leader.

To Jeremy Anderson, thank you for being an inspirational human being. I've been blessed to have you as a speaking coach and want to say I appreciate you so much.

To Anthony Flynn, thank you for being the best business coach and life guide. I'm grateful for all of the wisdom you have shared with me.

To all of the Next Level family—you all rock! I'm so proud to be a part of a group of world changers who are working on impacting the globe in a positive way.

Thank you to Eli Gonzalez and his team for all your help during the editing process. It is always so fantastic to work with you and your team.

Thank you to Adroit Solutions for all of their help over the years with partnering to help spread joy to various global communities. You all are the best!

A huge thank you to the entire BBG team, especially Jeremy Weber, Jay Twining, Briana Medford, and Jeff Mohs. Thanks for all of your wisdom and guidance throughout the writing and publishing of this book. So grateful to you all.

Thank you kindly to Dr. Shahana Alibhai, Dr. Akeia Keith, and Dr. Jacqueline King for writing such beautiful testimonials about the book. I appreciate your support more than you know!

Thank you to Joey Clay for dedicating your time and expertise to capture my author photos. Your remarkable photography skills are truly valued, and I appreciate our collaboration over the years.

RESOURCES

These resources encompass a range of mental health needs and are available to individuals across the United States. *Please note the author does not endorse any of these organizations nor makes any promises about the effectiveness of the help from these organizations.*

These are simply a suggested list of resources, not an exhaustive list, so please do your own research.

- **American Psychological Association (APA)**: Provides resources, articles, and information on finding a psychologist. https://www.apa.org/
- **National Alliance on Mental Illness (NAMI)**: Offers education, support groups, and advocacy for individuals and families affected by mental illness. https://www.nami.org/
- **Substance Abuse and Mental Health Services Administration (SAMHSA)**: Provides resources, treatment locators, and support for mental health and substance abuse issues. https://www.samhsa.gov/

RESOURCES

- **National Suicide Prevention Lifeline**: Offers free, confidential support and crisis intervention for individuals in distress. (1-800-273-TALK) https://suicidepreventionlifeline.org/
- **Crisis Text Line**: Provides free, confidential support via text messaging 24/7. Text HOME to 741741 to connect with a trained crisis counselor. https://www.crisistextline.org/
- **Psychology Today Therapist Directory**: Helps you find licensed therapists, psychiatrists, and treatment centers in your area. https://www.psychologytoday.com/us/therapists
- **MentalHealth.gov**: Offers information on mental health conditions, treatment options, and resources for seeking help. https://www.mentalhealth.gov/
- **National Institute of Mental Health (NIMH)**: Offers information on mental health disorders, research updates, and treatment options. https://www.nimh.nih.gov/
- **Anxiety and Depression Association of America (ADAA)**: Provides resources, support groups, and educational materials for anxiety and depression. https://adaa.org/
- **Mental Health America (MHA)**: Offers screening tools, educational resources, and advocacy for mental health awareness. https://www.mhanational.org/
- **National Eating Disorders Association (NEDA)**: Provides support, resources, and treatment referrals for individuals with eating disorders. https://www.nationaleatingdisorders.org/
- **Depression and Bipolar Support Alliance (DBSA)**: Offers support groups, educational resources, and advocacy for individuals with mood disorders. https://www.dbsalliance.org/

RESOURCES

- **SAMHSA's National Helpline**: Provides 24/7, free, and confidential treatment referral and information service for mental health and substance use disorders. (1-800-662-HELP) https://www.samhsa.gov/find-help/national-helpline
- **The Trevor Project**: Offers crisis intervention and suicide prevention services for LGBTQ+ youth. (1-866-488-7386) https://www.thetrevorproject.org/
- **Veterans Crisis Line**: Provides support for veterans in crisis and their families. (1-800-273-8255, press 1) https://www.veteranscrisisline.net/
- **The Recovery Village**: Offers resources and treatment options for individuals struggling with addiction and mental health disorders. https://www.therecoveryvillage.com/
- **American Foundation for Suicide Prevention (AFSP)**: Provides education, advocacy, and support for suicide prevention. https://afsp.org/
- **211**: Offers information and referrals for community resources, including mental health services, housing assistance, and more. https://www.211.org/
- **SAMHSA Disaster Distress Helpline**: Provides crisis counseling and support for individuals experiencing emotional distress related to natural or human-caused disasters. (1-800-985-5990) https://www.samhsa.gov/find-help/disaster-distress-helpline
- **The Jed Foundation**: Focuses on promoting emotional health and preventing suicide among college students. https://www.jedfoundation.org/
- **National Center for PTSD**: Provides resources, educational materials, and treatment options for individuals with post-traumatic stress disorder. https://www.ptsd.va.gov/

RESOURCES

- **Child Mind Institute**: Offers resources, articles, and support for children and families struggling with mental health issues. https://childmind.org/
- **The Steve Fund**: Focuses on supporting the mental health and emotional well-being of students of color. https://www.stevefund.org/
- **Active Minds**: Aims to reduce the stigma surrounding mental health on college campuses and provides resources for students. https://www.activeminds.org/
- **The National Domestic Violence Hotline**: Offers support and resources for individuals experiencing domestic violence. (1-800-799-SAFE) https://www.thehotline.org/
- **RAINN (Rape, Abuse & Incest National Network)**: Provides support for survivors of sexual assault and their loved ones. (1-800-656-HOPE) https://www.rainn.org/
- **Partnership for Drug-Free Kids**: Offers support, resources, and guidance for parents dealing with substance abuse and mental health issues in their children. https://drugfree.org/
- **The National Association of Free and Charitable Clinics**: Provides access to free or low-cost healthcare, including mental health services, for uninsured or underinsured individuals. https://www.nafcclinics.org/
- **The American Association of Suicidology (AAS)**: Offers resources, training, and support for professionals working in suicide prevention and intervention. https://suicidology.org/
- **Online Therapy Platforms**: Websites like BetterHelp, Talkspace, and 7 Cups offer online therapy and counseling services, making mental health support more accessible. BetterHelp: https://www.betterhelp.com/ Talkspace: https://www.talkspace.com/ 7 Cups: https://www.7cups.com/

SUPPORT GROUPS

These organizations provide support groups and resources tailored to specific mental health conditions and challenges, helping individuals and families across the United States.

- **National Alliance on Mental Illness (NAMI)**: NAMI provides education, support, and advocacy for individuals and families affected by mental illness. Their website offers resources, information on mental health conditions, and support group locators. https://www.nami.org/
- **Depression and Bipolar Support Alliance (DBSA)**: DBSA offers support groups, educational resources, and advocacy for individuals living with depression and bipolar disorder. Their website provides information on mood disorders and tools for managing symptoms. https://www.dbsalliance.org/
- **Anxiety and Depression Association of America (ADAA)**: ADAA offers resources, support groups, and

educational materials for anxiety and depression. Their website provides information on treatment options, self-help strategies, and finding mental health professionals. https://adaa.org/
- **Mental Health America (MHA)**: MHA offers screening tools, educational resources, and advocacy for mental health awareness. Their website provides information on mental health conditions, finding help, and taking action for mental health reform. https://www.mhanational.org/
- **Alcoholics Anonymous (AA)**: AA offers support groups and resources for individuals recovering from alcohol addiction. Their website provides information on the 12-step program, finding meetings, and connecting with a sponsor. https://www.aa.org/
- **Narcotics Anonymous (NA)**: NA provides support groups and resources for individuals recovering from drug addiction. Their website offers information on the 12-step program, finding meetings, and literature on recovery. https://www.na.org/
- **Smart Recovery**: Smart Recovery offers support groups and resources for individuals recovering from addiction to drugs, alcohol, or other substances. Their website provides information on the Smart Recovery program, finding meetings, and online resources. https://www.smartrecovery.org/
- **Emotions Anonymous (EA)**: EA offers support groups and resources for individuals seeking emotional support and recovery from mental health issues. Their website provides information on the EA program, finding meetings, and literature on emotional wellness. https://emotionsanonymous.org/
- **Al-Anon Family Groups**: Al-Anon offers support groups and resources for individuals affected by someone else's

alcohol addiction. Their website provides information on the Al-Anon program, finding meetings, and literature on coping with a loved one's addiction. https://al-anon.org/
- **Gamblers Anonymous (GA)**: GA offers support groups and resources for individuals recovering from gambling addiction. Their website provides information on the GA program, finding meetings, and literature on recovery from compulsive gambling. https://www.gamblersanonymous.org/
- **Dual Recovery Anonymous (DRA)**: DRA offers support groups and resources for individuals recovering from co-occurring substance use and mental health disorders. Their website provides information on the DRA program, finding meetings, and literature on dual recovery. https://draonline.org/
- **National Eating Disorders Association (NEDA)**: NEDA offers support, resources, and advocacy for individuals affected by eating disorders. Their website provides information on eating disorders, treatment options, and ways to get involved. https://www.nationaleatingdisorders.org/
- **Schizophrenia and Related Disorders Alliance of America (SARDAA)**: SARDAA offers support, resources, and advocacy for individuals living with schizophrenia and related disorders. Their website provides information on schizophrenia, treatment options, and support for caregivers. https://www.sardaa.org/
- **National Alliance for Grieving Children (NAGC)**: NAGC provides resources, education, and support for children and families coping with grief and loss. Their website offers information on grief support services, resources for professionals, and ways to get involved. https://childrengrieve.org/

SUPPORT GROUPS

- **The Compassionate Friends**: The Compassionate Friends offers support, resources, and community for bereaved parents and families who have experienced the death of a child. Their website provides information on grief support groups, online resources, and events. https://www.compassionatefriends.org/
- **Overeaters Anonymous (OA)**: OA offers support groups and resources for individuals recovering from compulsive overeating, binge eating, and other eating disorders. Their website provides information on the OA program, finding meetings, and literature on recovery. https://oa.org/
- **Adult Children of Alcoholics (ACA)**: ACA offers support groups and resources for adults who grew up in dysfunctional or alcoholic families. Their website provides information on ACA meetings, literature on recovery, and ways to connect with others in recovery. https://adultchildren.org/
- **National Association for Children of Alcoholics (NACoA)**: NACoA offers support, resources, and advocacy for children of alcoholics and their families. Their website provides information on resources for children and families, educational materials, and ways to get involved. https://nacoa.org/
- **Families for Depression Awareness**: Families for Depression Awareness offers education, support, and advocacy for families coping with depression and bipolar disorder. Their website provides information on mood disorders, tools for families, and ways to support loved ones. https://www.familyaware.org/
- **National Alliance for the Mentally Illness (NAMI) Connection**: NAMI Connection offers peer support groups for individuals living with mental illness. Their

SUPPORT GROUPS

website provides information on NAMI Connection groups, meeting schedules, and ways to get involved in peer support. https://www.nami.org/Support-Education/Support-Groups

Printed in the USA
CPSIA information can be obtained
at www.ICGtesting.com
LVHW022138110924
790842LV00026B/603